Creating Templates with Artisteer

Design professional-looking websites and CMS templates, on your own!

Jakub Sanecki

BIRMINGHAM - MUMBAI

Creating Templates with Artisteer

Copyright © 2013 Packt Publishing

First published: March 2013

Production Reference: 1120313

Published by Packt Publishing Ltd.
Livery Place
35 Livery Street
Birmingham B3 2PB, UK.

ISBN 978-1-84969-941-9

www.packtpub.com

Cover Image by Suresh Mogre (suresh.mogre.99@gmail.com)

Credits

Author
Jakub Sanecki

Reviewer
Mark Conroy

Acquisition Editor
Mary Nadar

Commissioning Editor
Priyanka Shah

Technical Editors
Charmaine Pereira

Amit Ramadas

Copy Editors
Laxmi Subramanian

Ruta Waghmare

Project Coordinator
Sneha Modi

Proofreader
Martin Diver

Indexer
Monica Ajmera

Graphics
Aditi Gajjar

Production Coordinator
Shantanu Zagade

Cover Work
Shantanu Zagade

About the Author

Jakub Sanecki is an experienced web developer and programmer, with over 11 years of experience. He was born in 1977 in Poland. In 2001, right before graduation (he graduated in company management) he founded Fregata—a company where he works until today, and took up his true passion, information technology. Starting with providing services related to a popular ERP system, the company evolved in the direction of programming services and custom software development. With the increasing popularity of the Internet, it concentrated on web applications' and websites' development. Author of many web and desktop applications, Jakub works as an independent IT consultant and freelancer, realizing projects of various size and complexity, for companies of various sizes. He also provides training courses related to IT and web technologies and the techniques to use them in the company environment. For some years he worked as a university teacher, teaching web and desktop programming.

Fregata is an authorized reseller of Extensoft. You can visit `www.szablonik.net`, as it provides support and additional information about this software tool.

Privately, a husband and father of two children, Jakub lives with his family in Sosnowiec (in Poland), spending little moments of free time playing piano or reading books.

Acknowledgement

Almost every book starts with some words, in which the authors thank people who have supported him/her and allowed him/her to finish the writing of the book. Following this nice and proper tradition, I would also like to thank the people, without whom this book would not have come into existence. First of all, I would like to thank to my wife, Hania, who supported me all the time and forgave all my whims while I was writing, taking care of our home and our son, and forgiving me for spending less time with them.

I would like to thank my parents who bought me my first computers and who always took care and trusted in me, even if my decisions seemed controversial to them. Without their acceptance and trust, I couldn't have realized my passion and started to make a living by founding a small IT company.

I would like to thank the rest of my family and my friends, for their patience and understanding while I was writing, as I didn't find time to meet them.

Last but not least, I would like to thank the people from Packt Publishing, who gave me a chance to write this book and did a great job, spending a lot of their time and work by correcting my initial drafts and providing valuable suggestions. Without their experience, knowledge, and commitment, I wouldn't have been able to finish this project.

About the Reviewer

Mark Conroy is a web developer and public speaker based in Galway, Ireland. A former English teacher by profession, he began designing websites as a hobby for friends' bands and local community groups. Since his humble beginning with Adobe Dreamweaver, he has graduated to working, almost exclusively, with Drupal, embracing open source technology whenever possible. As a speaker, he mostly presents on uses of digital media for effective campaigning. He has also presented at Drupal for Government days in Dublin on creating social networks using Drupal. Mark is a co-organizer of the monthly Galway Drupal Meetup.

As a freelance developer working under the name A Design For Life—www.adesignforlife.net, Mark has worked on a number of large projects, not least of which was the redevelopment of the Ireland Reaching Out website (www.irelandxo.com) that he built single-handedly from the ground up, using a combination of Drupal Commons (and some extra contributed Drupal modules), Artisteer, CSS, and CiviCRM. All functionality on the site was completed using innovative approaches to pre-existing modules from drupal.org. He also built and continues to maintain the political campaigns and contacts website contact.ie, which has become the most popular online method for contacting politicians in Ireland.

This is the first technical book Mark has worked on. He has, however, published a textbook for English students, *In Transition: An Anthology of Texts and Tasks for Transition Year Students*, is awaiting publication of a second English textbook, and is about to start work on his third.

Mark is available for long and/or short-term freelance work, especially in the area of Drupal and campaign technologies. You can contact him at info@adesignforlife.net or info@contact.ie.

www.PacktPub.com

Support files, eBooks, discount offers and more

You might want to visit www.PacktPub.com for support files and downloads related to your book.

Did you know that Packt offers eBook versions of every book published, with PDF and ePub files available? You can upgrade to the eBook version at www.PacktPub.com and as a print book customer, you are entitled to a discount on the eBook copy. Get in touch with us at service@packtpub.com for more details.

At www.PacktPub.com, you can also read a collection of free technical articles, sign up for a range of free newsletters and receive exclusive discounts and offers on Packt books and eBooks.

http://PacktLib.PacktPub.com

Do you need instant solutions to your IT questions? PacktLib is Packt's online digital book library. Here, you can access, read and search across Packt's entire library of books.

Why Subscribe?

- Fully searchable across every book published by Packt
- Copy and paste, print and bookmark content
- On demand and accessible via web browser

Free Access for Packt account holders

If you have an account with Packt at www.PacktPub.com, you can use this to access PacktLib today and view nine entirely free books. Simply use your login credentials for immediate access.

Table of Contents

Preface

Designing good-looking, professional-quality web templates or building your own website is a complicated task. Artisteer has changed this situation, enabling anyone to do it by themselves, without the need to learn things such as HTML, web-programming languages, or drawing. *Creating Templates with Artisteer* is a practical, step-by-step guide that will show you how to prepare an elegant, professional-looking website on your own, using the features of Artisteer.

This book is great for enthusiasts, Artisteer users, and individuals who want to create professional-looking websites without paying for professional services, expensive tools, and also to speed up the work and automate time-consuming tasks.

What this book covers

Chapter 1, Meet the Artisteer, helps you to learn what Artisteer exactly is and how it can be useful for you. We will familiarize you with the interface and some basic functions of the application. You will also prepare your very first template.

Chapter 2, The Template Step-by-Step, covers the typical process of designing with Artisteer, explaining all the typical elements of the template one by one. At the end of this chapter, you will be able to prepare your simple website all alone.

Chapter 3, CMS Templates, discusses advantages of using a content management system (CMS) over a static website, and how to use Artisteer for designing templates for such solutions. We will convert our example project into Joomla! and WordPress installable packages, and also import the content from Artisteer into CMS.

Chapter 4, Tips and Tricks, shows you some additional effects you can enrich your project with by slightly modifying the source code generated by the program.

What you need for this book

In order to appreciate this book completely, we recommend you to have Version 4 of Artisteer, which can be downloaded from http://www.artisteer.com/, and Notepad++, which can be downloaded from http://notepad-plus-plus.org/.

Who this book is for

This book is addressed to anyone wanting to build their private or company website on their own, without learning technical stuff such as HTML, CSS, or programming, and for professionals considering including Artisteer into their toolkit. It's also addressed to all the less-advanced Artisteer users, looking for a printed guide.

Conventions

In this book, you will find a number of styles of text that distinguish between different kinds of information. Here are some examples of these styles, and an explanation of their meaning.

Code words in text are shown as follows: "Edit the `template.css` file once again and append the following code at the end:"

A block of code is set as follows:

```
.customart-nostyle.MySpecialModule
{
  margin-top: 0;
  border: none;
}
```

New terms and **important words** are shown in bold. Words that you see on the screen, in menus or dialog boxes for example, appear in the text like this: "Choose the **Colors & Fonts** tab on the ribbon.".

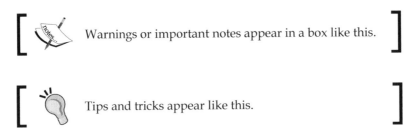

Warnings or important notes appear in a box like this.

Tips and tricks appear like this.

Reader feedback

Feedback from our readers is always welcome. Let us know what you think about this book—what you liked or may have disliked. Reader feedback is important for us to develop titles that you really get the most out of.

To send us general feedback, simply send an e-mail to feedback@packtpub.com, and mention the book title via the subject of your message.

If there is a topic that you have expertise in and you are interested in either writing or contributing to a book, see our author guide on www.packtpub.com/authors.

Customer support

Now that you are the proud owner of a Packt book, we have a number of things to help you to get the most from your purchase.

Downloading the example code

You can download the example code files for all Packt books you have purchased from your account at http://www.packtpub.com. If you purchased this book elsewhere, you can visit http://www.packtpub.com/support and register to have the files e-mailed directly to you.

Errata

Although we have taken every care to ensure the accuracy of our content, mistakes do happen. If you find a mistake in one of our books—maybe a mistake in the text or the code—we would be grateful if you would report this to us. By doing so, you can save other readers from frustration and help us improve subsequent versions of this book. If you find any errata, please report them by visiting http://www.packtpub.com/submit-errata, selecting your book, clicking on the **errata submission form** link, and entering the details of your errata. Once your errata are verified, your submission will be accepted and the errata will be uploaded on our website, or added to any list of existing errata, under the Errata section of that title. Any existing errata can be viewed by selecting your title from http://www.packtpub.com/support.

Piracy

Piracy of copyright material on the Internet is an ongoing problem across all media. At Packt, we take the protection of our copyright and licenses very seriously. If you come across any illegal copies of our works, in any form, on the Internet, please provide us with the location address or website name immediately so that we can pursue a remedy.

Please contact us at copyright@packtpub.com with a link to the suspected pirated material.

We appreciate your help in protecting our authors, and our ability to bring you valuable content.

Questions

You can contact us at questions@packtpub.com if you are having a problem with any aspect of the book, and we will do our best to address it.

1
Meet the Artisteer

In this book, you will see that you are able to design and prepare a professional-quality website template all alone, without anybody's help. You don't need to know how to draw or how to code. You don't need to worry about HTML, CSS, PHP, and all that complicated stuff. All you need is your copy of Artisteer.

You may ask, "What is Artisteer?"

What is Artisteer

Artisteer is an Automated Web Designer. What does it mean? In simple words, it's an application that lets you prepare great websites, even if you don't know anything about drawing, programming, web technology, and all that stuff. With Artisteer, you can design your website, fill it with content, and in the end, generate the ready-to-use HTML/CSS files that you can upload to your web server (in fact, this can also be done in Artisteer). You can also automatically generate any layout in the form of a template dedicated to one of several well-known CMS systems, such as Joomla!, Drupal, WordPress, or DotNetNuke. The design process looks totally different in comparison to the traditional way in which it's usually done. While you still have a lot of control and can decide many aspects of your design, the drawing process is done automatically and doesn't demand any graphic skills from you, except a good eye for what looks good on a page. And it's fast. Indeed very, very fast.

Artisteer was the first application of its kind in the market and still remains one of the best tools in this category.

Artisteer versus other software tools

Because Artisteer is a new kind of tool, it is hard to give a proper definition of what it is. There are a lot of easier ways to say what Artisteer is not. This will allow us to avoid any confusion about what it should be compared with. If we consider the typical process of building a website, it usually consists of several stages as follows:

1. Firstly, a designer prepares a design. He usually works with a graphics editor.

2. When the design is ready, it's analyzed in detail to qualify what can be achieved with HTML/CSS, and what has to stay as pictures. Then the whole layout is sliced into small pictures.

3. A web developer prepares the layout in the HTML language and places every single picture into its proper position with the help of CSS. To illustrate the look of the site and to be able to choose the appropriate typography, the places for content are usually filled with some dummy text (for example, `Lorem ipsum dolor sit amet...`). He does this usually with a code editor.

4. The dummy text gets replaced with the target content. This task is usually done with the help of a WYSIWYG editor. At the end of this stage, we have a complete static website.

5. If the website should contain some more sophisticated elements, such as photo galleries, fancy tooltips, movies, forms, and so on, or if it should be transformed into a template for a CMS, an additional code has to be written. This is the job of a programmer, who writes the code in a code editor using a client-side or server-side language (according to what should be achieved).

This allocation of tasks is of course quite hypothetical, and it may vary in particular teams and companies, but the goal was to show you the flow of the overall process. Sometimes the entire process is done by a single person, but in the case of bigger projects, it's not uncommon that every stage is realized by a group of people. Therefore, we're talking about a group of people (a team of various specialists) using different tools, such as graphics editors, WYSIWYG HTML editors, code editors, and so on.

- Artisteer is not a graphics editor. In a graphics editor, you must design everything by hand, while in Artisteer all the elements (for example, header, menu, and so on) are generated automatically, according to the parameters you set via the program's interface. Graphic editors offer sophisticated tools, which Artisteer doesn't contain, to process pictures and photos. In a graphics editor you can create any graphic, while in Artisteer the only thing you can design is a website.

- Artisteer is not a WYSIWYG editor. In a **What You See Is What You Get (WYSIWYG)** editor, you can type the words and insert the graphic elements into a website in a similar way as you would use a word processor (for example, MS Word) and the application automatically transforms everything into an HTML code. The layout elements in Artisteer are not just graphics, they are highly interactive and you have a lot of control over them. You can resize them, change the color, border, placement, and almost any other aspect of their look and feel. Your actions are not transformed into HTML immediately. You work with a binary Artisteer project (`.artx` files), and only when you press the **Export** button, the layout is exported. What it means is that all the layout is processed in one go and the HTML/CSS/JavaScript/PHP code is generated. But it's also true, that the way of working with Artisteer is practically WYSIWYG—you don't see any code, but the final design.

- Artisteer is not a code editor. You can press the **Show the code** button and take a look at the HTML file that will be generated (and even change it), but this is not the native way you will work with this application. The native way is "point and click". In a code editor you write the code and preview the results. In Artisteer you modify the results and preview the generated code.

- Artisteer is also not a collection of predesigned layouts, as many people seem to think. There is no upper limit on the unique layouts that can be created, because the answer is unlimited. It's true that the program contains a limited number of graphics and predefined elements, for example, menu. But the possibility of inserting your own images and determining almost any aspect of the elements (size, colors, fonts, and so on) suggests that you are a real designer, and not just someone who selects a template from the predefined options.

The tools that are most similar to Artisteer are other web builder applications. The difference is in what you can change and set up. As I mentioned earlier, you can change almost everything in Artisteer.

Who can use Artisteer

So who is Artisteer dedicated to? The potential audience of this program is very large. I can't be sure, but I feel that the intention of Artisteer's creators was to create a tool that allows the nongraphic and nontechnician people to create complete and great-looking websites. This would place Artisteer as a tool for hobbyists and enthusiasts, but the scope of users is much larger. Let's consider this problem from several different points of view.

Hobbyists

A hobbyist is somebody who wants to have a website because of his/her private passion. It's not his/her job, it's not his/her business, he/she won't gain any money on it. It may be a private blog on Blogger or WordPress, or just a simple family website, often based on the cheapest hosting service possible. For such a person, hiring a professional web development company or freelancer is usually not an option because of the cost. Usually, the only available option is to try to prepare the page on his/her own (the results will be adequate to his/her skills), or to buy a ready-made template (accepting the fact that there are a lot of different websites that look the same). Artisteer gives such people a third option: buy the program and prepare a unique and good-looking site all alone. The cost will be less than the usual price for a ready-made, standard layout on the market.

Designers

A designer is an artistically talented person who can use the graphics editors and create good-looking designs for web pages. In a team, a designer usually does the first stage of work, creating an overall concept of how the site will look, and preparing the graphics. While a designer is good at drawing, he/she can't code. To create a website a designer needs the help of a web developer. But with Artisteer, he/she can design the template and enrich it with his/her own custom graphic elements, which he/she can prepare. He/she can even enter the content and transfer this all into a CMS skin, offering the end user a complete solution.

Web developers and programmers

The frontier that divides web developers and programmers is often very thin, and various companies use different names for the same jobs. In this book, we assume that a web developer is someone with the skills for creating HTML/CSS code. Additionally, he or she often has good knowledge of administrating the CMSs, can install and configure various extensions, and is able to prepare the whole website, including stylesheet modifications, as there's no requirement of individual programming. The programmers are usually "next-level web developers", with programming skills. Usually, they code the core of the CMS systems or its additional functionality (create extensions). In short, we can assume that a web developer is someone who builds websites using the things that a programmer codes.

Web developers and programmers are able to build the whole website on their own, if not for one problem—they can't draw. They may be great technicians, but not graphics designers, and even the most technically advanced site without graphics does not impress anybody. That's why they often use ready-made templates as a basis for further work. The problem arises when there is a need to modify not the functionality, but the look of the site. In that case they have to cooperate with the designers.

Designers are the people who have an artistic taste. They can assess what looks good and what doesn't, even if they couldn't draw it on their own. Artisteer offers them the possibility to design a template independently, by determining the look of the site and its various elements, by changing their parameters such as colors, position, size, and so on. As you will see later, working with Artisteer resembles a situation wherein the designer is sitting next to you, listening to your suggestions, making the changes on the fly, and presenting the results immediately.

Web development companies

One of the main reasons that people work together is that nobody is perfect, nobody possesses all the talent. It would seem that for an individual, Artisteer may be a good option, because it allows him to avoid cooperation (which can be costly) with other specialists and to create the whole project alone. But in case of a team consisting of people with different complementary skills, there's no need to use such a tool at all. Based on my personal experience, I disagree with such a thought, and I can quote several arguments to support my words as follows:

- The main cost factors of any work or project is always the time and the skills required for the job to be done. Designing and programming are very time-consuming tasks, and any automation saves time and money.

- One of the biggest and most frustrating things in the web-design business is that your customer usually won't pay for something that he or she hasn't seen before. With Artisteer, the first stage of concept can really be done very fast.

The previously discussed examples of why Artisteer can be useful for various groups of people doesn't mean that everything be done with Artisteer, of course. For example, you can't add any logic to the site, as this would demand a programming work. Similarly with the graphics, even the best automated generator won't replace the real artist. Like with every other thing, the custom and handmade products are the best, and websites are not an exception to this. For example, cars. Do you agree that a representative, handmade limousine, or a sports car is better than a popular compact from serial production? You probably do, but do you have a handmade sports car? Millions of people everyday drive the cheap compacts to commute, and they are pretty happy with it. Price is the factor. The same is with websites.

Your first template in 10 minutes

Ok, enough of just talking. Let's see Artisteer in action. Like in most programming books, where the first exercise is displaying the "Hello World!" text, we are going to create our first "Hello World!" template. So let's begin.

The program comes in two editions: Home & Academic and Standard, which differ in functionality. The Home & Academic edition is a truncated version of the Standard edition. In this book we work with the Standard edition.

You can download the latest version from the producer's website under the address `http://www.artisteer.com/?p=downloads`. There is one installer for both the versions and according to the license number you have, the Standard or Home & Academic edition will be activated. The same installer can also be used to install the trial version that allows you to know the program and make the decision if you want to buy it or not.

The trial version has no time limit for usage or feature limitations. You may use it for as long as you wish and play with all functionalities. The difference between the trial and full versions is that the trial version doesn't allow you to save a project, and the exported templates show the **Trial** watermark.

The installation process is fully automated, and if you accept the license terms and don't need to install the application in a specific location, all you have to do is just click on the **Next** button until the process is finished.

To transform the trial version into the full version, the application needs to be activated. This process requires an Internet connection. To activate, click on the **Activate** button shown on the welcome screen (you can also choose the **File** | **Activation** option from the menu). You will go to the **Artisteer Activation** window, where you should enter your license key into the **License Key:** field", as shown in the following screenshot:

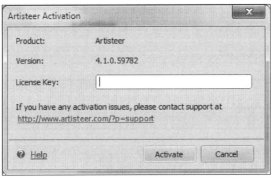

Activation window

After you have entered your license key, click on the **Activate** button. After a few seconds, your copy of Artisteer will be fully activated.

Creating a new project

After you start the program, the first screen you will see is a window titled **New Project**. Here you can decide whether you want to open a previously saved project, or start a new one. The main part of this window consists of three rows. In the first row you can filter among the available, pre-made templates (if you want to start by modifying one of them). The pre-made templates are presented in the third row, according to which category and sorting rule you choose.

The second row always contains only one icon. Click on it when you want to start with a **Blank** template and style everything from scratch.

In the column to the right-hand side of the window, there is a list of recently opened projects, as in the following screenshot:

The startup window in Artisteer

You may say, "Wait a minute! You have said that in Artisteer I can design not only static websites, but also templates for various CMSs. Where can I set up what exactly I'm going to do?" Yes, you are right. What's more, in the previous versions of Artisteer, there was an additional field in the startup window where you could set it up. But with the current version, you don't have such an option. It's not a restriction of functionality, but rather a change in the philosophy of working with the application. You are just designing, no matter which platform you will choose later. That's because you choose the platform at the end, not at the beginning. It also highlights the fact that Artisteer enables you to focus on the design, and not the platform that you choose. Think of design as something that is platform independent.

Because we want to start with a blank template, let's click on the solitary icon in the second row. Artisteer will load its default data. In the following steps we are going to turn it into our custom layout.

As you can see, the **Blank** template is not really empty. It contains some basic elements and some example content. However, this is the most initial state while working with Artisteer, used when you are going to design a template from scratch.

The program interface

What you see in the next screenshot is Artisteer's default interface. If you're familiar with modern applications, you will feel right at home. The main menu is in the form of a ribbon (introduced in Microsoft Office 2007), and the main options, such as **Edit**, **Colors & Fonts**, **Layout**, **Content**, **Background**, **Sheet**, **Header**, **Menu**, **Blocks**, **Vertical Menu**, **Controls**, and **Footer** correspond to the main stages while designing a layout (we will talk about those things in detail in the next chapter). The first option, called **Home**, contains the options that affect the whole site in general.

Are you a little bit confused about how to start? Don't worry! Before we use the more advanced options, we will start with a very simple and intuitive tool: the Suggest Mode function.

Program interface

The Suggestion tool

Suggest Mode is a function that suggests a look of the element you are currently working on. Because the **Home** tab refers to the scope of the whole project, using this function at this level suggests the whole design with all the dependent elements. Let's click on the icon. It's the yellow bulb, first on the left, with the **Suggest Design** label.

The whole design has changed. Amazing, isn't it? It's not just switching to the next available template from a collection. When you clicked on the icon, Artisteer generated a whole new layout, consisting of randomly generated elements. What you see is unique. If you don't believe it, you can very easily test it on your own. Just restart the program and try to do it once again. You will probably never see exactly the same layout twice.

Click over and over on the **Suggest Design** icon, until you really like what you see.

What's interesting is that although a new proposal is generated every time randomly, the **Undo** function works correctly. It seems that the full history of generated layouts is stored as long as the program runs.

Previewing the project

At any time, you can see the live preview of your project in the browser. To get it, perform the following steps:

1. Click on the **File** menu (above the ribbon).
2. Choose the **Preview In Browser** function. A list of browsers installed in your system will expand.
3. Choose the browser you want to see your project in.

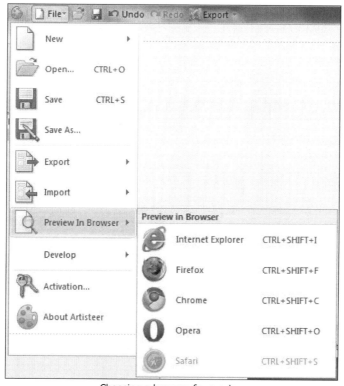

Choosing a browser for preview

After a while the selected browser will open, showing your project in its current state. Look at the address bar. You will notice that what you see is a real HTML file that was generated by the program (in your system's temporary directory). It's important because you can be sure that you see exactly the same file that will be generated while exporting the project.

Initial customizations

If you are satisfied with the project, double-click on the **Enter Site Title** text (sometimes it can also be **Best Idea** or something else, but it's always the biggest text in the header). You will see the blinking cursor, like in any word processor. Delete the text and type Hello World!. Do the same with the site slogan below the header, replacing the original text with My first Artisteer template. After you have finished typing, just click on any other element to apply the changes.

On the left-hand side of the screen you can see a panel named the **Pages** section. That is where you define the number and titles of pages your entire site contains. Please note that the content of this panel is strictly connected with the menus in your project. By default, every project has two menus—a horizontal and a vertical one. Both the menus are pretty interactive even while designing. For example, if you move your mouse cursor over the first position of the horizontal menu, it will expand, showing all containing subpositions. The vertical menu behaves similarly, but you must click on the position to expand it.

When you click on the menu item, the corresponding page in the **Pages** section on the left panel will be selected. The panel presents all the pages in the form of a tree. You can click on the little triangle on the left of the **Home** page to expand its child elements. You can observe that at the beginning, Artisteer creates both the menus with two positions in them, and the first position contains tree subpositions.

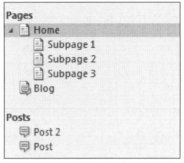

Pages are presented in the form of a tree,
showing the structure of the project

A small website usually has only one menu—vertical or horizontal. If there's a need to use two (or more) menus, the first one is usually the main menu, and the second acts as its subordinate, displaying options on the lower levels. In our first project we don't need two menus, so we will preserve only the horizontal menu.

Let's change the titles of the menu's positions and the titles of the subpages of the site.

In the left panel, do the following:

1. The name of the first page, **Home**, is good. We will leave it unchanged.

2. Expand all the child elements of **Home** by clicking on the little triangle on the left.

3. Right-click on the **Subpage 1** item, and from the content menu choose **Rename**. The label will be selected and you can now delete the text and type. Type About Me and press *Enter*. Right-click on **Subpage 2** and rename it as Contact, as described above.

4. Right-click on **Subpage 3**, and from content menu choose **Delete**. On the confirmation dialog choose **Yes**.

5. Rename **Blog** as My Blog.

The structure of your project should now be as shown in the following screenshot:

Structure of our project after changes

The structure of menus has also changed according to the changes we made. The horizontal menu should look like the following screenshot:

Horizontal menu immediately presents
the current structure of the page

Now, click on the **Vertical Menu** group on the ribbon and click on **Position**. A list with the possible positions, where the vertical menu can be displayed, will expand. The vertical menu is displayed as the filled square. Let's choose the first option called **No Block**. This option does not display the vertical menu at all:

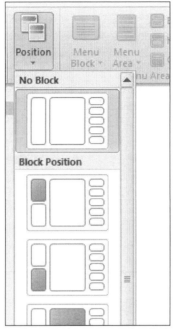

We set the vertical menu to not be displayed

Ok, we have finished our first design. It didn't take more than 10 minutes, did it? If so, try to do it once again. When you know what you're doing, I'm sure you can do it this time even more quickly.

Saving the project

You should archive every project (since you know that an Artisteer project not only contains a design, but also the content, we should call it a project rather than just a template) you have made. This simple principle may sound trivial, but there are many reasons to follow it, as follows:

- Whether you do the project for yourself or someone else, sooner or later there'll be a need to modify it

- You or your customer can make the decision of changing the CMS platform (but not the design)

- Your server may break, or be attacked

In all of the discussed situations, it will be suitable to have a copy of your work to modify or restore the website. The simplest (and I think the best) way to achieve this goal is to save the project in the native Artisteer binary format. That's right. Although Artisteer generates the templates as a set of HTML/CSS/JavaScript/PHP files (or one ZIP archive), it also has its own native binary file with the `.artx` extension. Those files contain all the components of your project design and its content.

 You may think of it as an analogy to writing a document in MS Word. The resulting form of a document is the printed sheets of paper, but you can save and archive your document in the form of a MS Word `.docx` file. Then you can load your `.docx` file into Word at any time, modify it, and print it once again. Printed sheets of paper are rather hard to change—it's possible only by hand, with a pencil. The same situation is with Artisteer and the exported web pages. You can open an `.artx` file at any time, make some changes, and export the template once again, but changing the exported files is possible only with manual coding. There is no way to reverse the export process and import the exported template back into Artisteer. It is also not possible to take, for example, a template from `drupal.org` and import it into Artisteer for editing.

To save your project, click on the icon on the shortcuts menu on the ribbon, or expand the **File** menu and choose the **Save** or **Save As...** option. Then type the name of your project, set the target location of the file (the default saving path is `C:\users\YourUser\Documents\Artisteer Templates`), and click on **Save**.

Note that Artisteer shows a list of the recent projects on startup; so the next time you start Artisteer, you will see your project on the list.

As I mentioned earlier, if you choose to store your projects in the form of HTML files, you can't open and edit the project with Artisteer anymore, and you'll have to code all the possible modifications manually. Even if you have a good understanding of how to do it, you can be sure that manual coding takes a lot more effort and time than working with Artisteer. There is also one more reason in favor of choosing the native files for your archive. The `.artx` files are independent of the CMS platforms. Let's say you run your site with WordPress and want to port it into Joomla! (or vice versa). No problem, you just open the `.artx` file and export it once again, choosing Joomla! as the target. If you had only the exported template files, to do such a migration, you would need to recode the whole template. Of course, here we skip the situation that you work on a more complicated project, in which Artisteer is used only as a middle tool, and the exported template undergoes further modifications to add some additional functionality. But in such cases, I'm sure you will decide to archive everything possible, for example, `.artx` files, source graphic files, read template, and so on.

Exporting the template

Now that we have designed and saved our project, it's time for exporting. To export the project, click on the **Export** icon on the shortcuts area of the ribbon, or choose **File | Export | Website Template** from the menu. We are going to export the project as a **Website Template** form. What it means is that this will be a static and normal website, not powered with any CMS system.

Exporting a project

In the window that appears as shown in the following screenshot, we have to set some parameters:

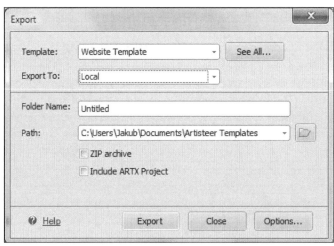

In the Export window, you set up export parameters

- **Template**: This is a field you can change to the desired type of exported template (CMS system). We leave it as it is, with **Website Template**.

- **Export to**: This is a field where you can determine if you want to export it to **Local** (as files on your hard drive) or **FTP** (transfer it directly into your web server). We want to export it as **Local**.

- **Folder Name**: This is the name of the folder that will be created, and in which all the template files will be saved. This name cannot contain spaces and characters that are forbidden when naming a folder (for example, \, /, ?, and so on). Let's delete the default value (**Untitled**) and type myFirstTemplate.

 Although Windows doesn't recognize small and big letters, Linux does, and your web server is probably powered by Linux. While naming the folder, be careful how you type its name.

- **Path**: This is the navigation path to the created folder. Click the browse icon and choose your desktop.

  Below, there are two additional options:

  - **ZIP archive**: If you check this checkbox, the template won't be saved in a new folder, but as a ZIP archive, with the name you typed in the **Folder Name** field. This option should be checked for most CMSs. Because we are not exporting to any CMS for now, we leave this option unchecked.

  - **Include ARTX Project**: If this option is checked, the binary Artisteer project file is saved among the other template files. I suggest that you leave it unchecked, as we have already saved our project.

 Most CMSs offer the functionality of installing templates in the form of ZIP archives that can be uploaded through its administrative panel. If you export for a CMS, you will probably check this option.

Removing the Footnote

Before we click on the **Export** button, we navigate to **Options** (click on that button). By default, Artisteer inserts a note in the footer, informing that this template was created with Artisteer. Since this is a clever marketing move from Extensoft (the company that produces Artisteer), in most cases you will not want to include such information.

In the **Options** window, click on the last position on the left-hand side (**Footnote**) and uncheck both the **Include a backward link to the Author** and **Include backward links to the CMS and the Artisteer** options as shown in the following screenshot:

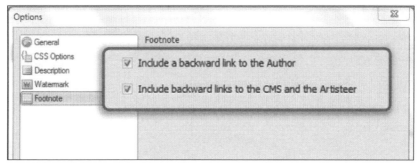

Remove the note about Artisteer, that is, Created with Artisteer, from the footer

Click on **OK** to return to the previous window, and click on **Export** to export the template. After a while, the process will be finished and you will find a new folder on your desktop: myFirstTemplate.

Congratulations! You have just designed, saved, and exported your first template in Artisteer. Open this folder and double-click on the index.html file. After a while, you'll see your site in your default browser.

Summary

In this chapter, you have learned what kind of tool Artisteer is, what is its place among other software tools, and how it can be useful for different groups of users. You now know how to create new projects, modify them using the Suggestion tool, and export them as working HTML websites.

You also know how to remove the **Created with Artisteer** note from the footer and how to save the project in the native Artisteer's file, for further modifications and backup purposes.

Now, you are ready to know the details of how to design a template with Artisteer.

2
The Template Step-by-Step

In the previous chapter, we discussed some overall features of Artisteer. So far, you have learned what the software is for and have acquired a little experience with its interface and work style.

Now we are going to prepare a template together. I will lead you through all the steps, from the beginning to the end. At the end of this chapter, you will have a complete template that you can directly implement for your website or modify to fulfill your needs. This will be a template for a static web page.

Templates

Before we can begin with creating a template, we have to define what exactly is a template.

A **template** is a set of common elements of the website. And you may then ask, what is a website? A **website** is a set of logically connected web pages, concerning one particular subject. When we talk about a company website, the subject will be the company. In case of a private website, the subject will be the person who the website is about, and so on.

You could, of course, design all the subpages individually with a different design for each of them. While this is possible, such a solution would have several serious disadvantages. They are listed as follows:

- If the pages don't have a consistent design and layout, visitors may get the impression that they have been redirected to another website and may feel lost
- If each page has a different, individual menu, located in different places, navigating between the pages would be difficult, and the visitor would have to focus on how to navigate instead of on the content
- The website will not look uniform throughout

To avoid such disadvantages (and to not leave the visitors confused), we have to make all the subpages look similar. This is achieved by the use of the same graphics elements (for example, the company logo on each subpage) and the same (or different, but consistent in some way) layout.

But it would be too little to say that the only element that should be common to all subpages is the company logo (in the case of a company website, of course). There are many elements that you can distinguish as a common part of a website. The combination of all of them together is a template.

 You may be under the impression that using a template restricts the creativity of the designer and reduces the individuality of particular subpages. While this is true, remember that the goal is to create a good website, not a single subpage. And the challenge for a designer is to create a good, individual template. You can compare it with cars: all cars have much in common. Cars have four wheels, a room for the driver and the passengers, an engine, a trunk, and so on. But do they all look the same? Certainly not. And now think of the different models of Porsche. Do they look similar enough to let everybody know it is a Porsche? I think so. Does it make a Porsche an ugly, unattractive car? Well, I wouldn't mind driving one!

The common parts of a website

It's time to try to distinguish the common parts of the website. We will divide them into **elements** and **attributes**.

Elements are those parts of a site that exist independently. I mean that you could replace them and those changes would not affect the rest of the site. An example of an element is a footer or a menu. You could change the look of the footer (color, font, or border) but it wouldn't affect the menu or any other element.

An attribute is something that affects the whole site (all elements). An example of an attribute is page width. If you decide to make your website wider or narrower, you will probably have to redesign all of the elements to fit into the new space. Think of the footer mentioned previously. The footer is usually as wide as the whole page. If you make the site wider, you have to make the footer wider too.

Elements

The list of elements may vary for particular websites, but in general we can distinguish them.

Header

A header is a container that identifies the site. It is usually as long as the whole page and is located at the top of the page. It's also the first element that you see while reading the page. According to the subject of the site, a header contains other elements in it, such as the company logo (on a company website), the author's photo (in a blog), a slogan, a picture of a product, or an image that refers to the content. A header can also contain some additional elements, such as language flags or contact data.

Horizontal menu

If a page has a horizontal menu, it's usually located either just below the header or above the footer. It is a navigation element, containing links to other pages.

Vertical menu

A vertical menu is a navigation element, usually located on the left or right side of a page. Like the horizontal menu, it contains links to other pages.

Content area

Content area is the place where you read content (information that you get from the page). It may contain text, pictures, galleries, movies, tables, forums, links, and any other kind of information you can publish on a website. Content area is the main and biggest part of the page.

Special blocks

Special blocks includes additional elements that may be required by some pages and that appear on all (or almost all) subpages, for example, a login form.

The division of what is an element and what is content is rather smooth and may vary in particular cases. We are trying to list the elements that are common for the whole site (they appear on all the subpages). Depending on your design, the same information can once be an element, while at another time, it can be just content. For example, consider a phone number. If you write it on the **Contact** page, in the content area, it is content. But you can also conclude that this is such an important piece of information that you want to display it on every page in a special **Contact** block, or even in the header. In that case, it will be an element. It's not uncommon either for information on a website to be both content and an element.

Footer

A footer is the last element of a page. It usually contains the copyright information. It may also contain the bottom menu, some additional information, and a backlink to the webmaster.

Attributes

Attributes are the characteristics that apply to the whole page. Typically we can distinguish them as follows:

Page width

There are many devices you can surf the Internet with: we have desktops, laptops, netbooks, tablets, smartphones, and so on. Each of these devices has a different screen size and resolution. This means that layout size is important. Your site should be displayed correctly on as many different devices as possible. This usually leads to a compromise. You shouldn't design your page too wide (making it look good, but only for the visitors with new, high-end monitors), but prepare it for a wider public, and also for those with older hardware. That's why the layouts are usually centered with an empty space or a background around it.

The first point of interest is the width. The height is not so important because you can scroll the site with the mouse without breaking the flow of reading, while horizontal scrolling is burdensome. Nevertheless, you shouldn't totally forget about the height either, especially when designing the header. Nowadays, screens are increasingly becoming panoramic, and it's not too good if your visitor can see only the header.

Typography

Typography is a set of fonts and its styles that appear on a page. You should avoid using different fonts on different subpages. Instead, the content on every subpage should be written with the same, consistent fonts. Just imagine reading a book in which every page is printed with different fonts. You would not think it was very professional, would you? According to the complexity of the content, you will have to define at least the font for the headers (titles), for the paragraphs (normal text), and for the hyperlinks. If your content is more sophisticated, you may need more header levels, table headers, table contents, quotations, and so on. Also, you shouldn't forget about line spacing and margins. Typography is an important part of design and can greatly improve or spoil the final effect.

Colors

The colors of all elements (their borders, backgrounds, and so on) should be chosen in such a way so as to create a coherent whole. We're going to call this set of colors a **color theme**. A color theme is a very important factor of any design because it can define the ambience of a whole website. The right color theme for a design is like the right rhythm for a song.

Layout

A layout is an arrangement of all the elements of the page. When talking about layout, we talk about the columns that a layout usually contains. A column is the vertical part of a page that can contain elements such as a vertical menu, special blocks, or a content area. The columns are usually located between the header and the footer.

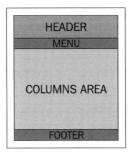

You can say that every layout has *at least one* column. Even if it seems that a layout doesn't contain any columns at all, in reality it's a one-column layout.

 Every layout has at least one column.

Remember that when we talk about a layout column, we do not talk about a column of text (in newspapers, the text is divided into several columns) but about separate areas (containers) of a page, where you can put elements. If a column contains a content area, the content can itself be divided into many columns, but this is still one column according to our definition.

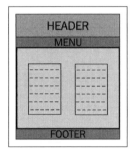

We can distinguish three typical layouts.

One-column layout

A one-column layout is usually used for blogs, private websites, and simple company websites. A one-column layout contains only a horizontal menu.

Two-column layout

The two-column layout is the most popular one. The first column usually contains a vertical menu, while the second one is used for displaying the content area. A two-column layout can contain a vertical menu, a horizontal menu, or both. If a two-column layout contains only a horizontal menu, the side column is used for additional blocks, for example, the login box. The following figure shows a two-column layout with a vertical menu on the left:

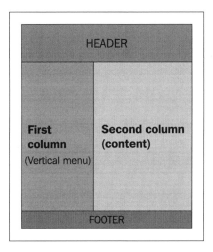

The following figure shows a two-column layout with a vertical menu on the right:

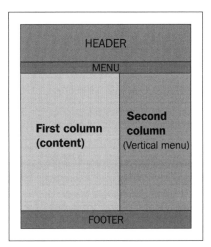

Three-column layout

The three-column layout is used usually for the more advanced websites. It consists of two side columns (usually left and right) and one large column in the middle. The side columns contain various special blocks and the middle column displays the content. The diagram for three-column layout is as follows:

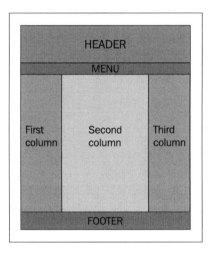

Creating a template

Now we are going to prepare our first layout. We will do this together, one step at a time, explaining every step we go through. But before we begin, let me first explain what we are going to achieve.

We are going to prepare a website advertising you as a web designer. The structure of the site is shown in the following diagram:

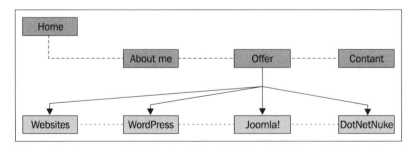

As you can see, our site will consist of eight pages. The first page (drawn a little bit above the other pages in the diagram) is the Home page. This is the first page that the visitor will see on coming to our site, and also the first page that we have to design. Logically, it is on the same level as the other pages from the first row. The second row shows the subpages for the Offer page. For our project we will create a two-column layout, with the first column on the left side, showing a vertical menu and a block with the contact information. Our site will have also a horizontal menu. Are you ready? If so, start Artisteer on the startup screen, click on the **Blank** template, and follow the next part of this chapter!

Unfortunately, in Artisteer you cannot set one menu to act as the submenu of another. Neither can you decide on which pages should the menu be displayed. Both the menus are displayed on all the pages. All you can do is decide which pages should be presented on which menu (after you add a new page into your project, it immediately appears in both the menus, but you can then exclude some of the pages). In our project, the ideal solution would be to make our vertical menu act as a submenu of the horizontal menu and show only the pages with our offer. This menu should be visible only when the Offer page is selected in the horizontal menu and is invisible on all the other pages. Such a thing is, alas, something that we are not able to achieve. Let's hope that the next version of Artisteer will be extended for such possibilities. Because we cannot do it this way, we are going to design both menus, and then you can decide which one you prefer to use and which should be deleted. We will also prepare a compromise solution that you may also find acceptable in this case.

To make the vertical menu act as a submenu is possible, but it requires a manual change of the exported code. In *Chapter 4*, *Tips and Tricks*, you can find a description of how to do this.

Fortunately, this limitation has no importance at all while using any old supported CMS platform.

To start with, our template looks like this:

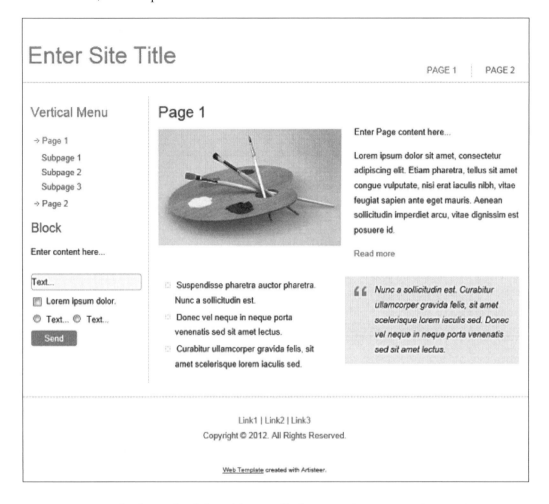

We are now on the first tab of the ribbon, called **Home**. It contains the **Design Ideas** area, **Website**, and **Export**. In **Design Ideas**, you can find different scopes of **Suggestion Tool**. The first button on the left is **Suggest Design**, and it fires automatic suggestions for the whole design. The next few buttons, **Suggest Colors**, **Suggest Fonts**, **Layout**, **Background**, and **Styles** fire automatic suggestions that change the appearance of the corresponding parts of the page.

The tabs on the ribbon group functions are logically connected with the tab's name. For example, all the buttons on the **Background** tab apply to the background of the page. The first tab, **Home**, is the parent tab.

It is also a rule that the first button on every tab is always **Suggestion Tool** for the elements that apply to the tab.

It so happens that the same function is available on different tabs. This is because some buttons logically apply to more than one tab. For example, the **Sheet Width** (on the **Layout** tab) and **Width** (on the **Sheet** tab) buttons are the same. Setting the width of the page is something that applies equally well to **Layout** and **Sheet**, so Artisteer's authors decided to put this option on both tabs.

Other buttons are used to add and delete pages and blog posts, insert special blocks, and to export the template quickly.

Layout

The first thing that we should set up while designing a new website is its width. If you are interested in creating web pages, you probably have a monitor with a large widescreen and good resolution. But we have to remember that not all of your visitors will have such good hardware. All the templates generated by Artisteer are centered, and almost all modern browsers enable you to freely zoom the page. It's far better to let some of your visitors enlarge the site than to make the rest of them use the horizontal scroll bar while reading.

The resolution you choose will depend on the target audience of your site. Usually, private computers have better parameters than the typical PCs used for just office work in companies. So if you design a site that you know will be viewed mostly by private individuals, you can choose a slightly wider layout than you might for a typical business site. But you cannot forget that many nonbusiness websites, such as community sites, are often accessed from offices.

So what is the answer? In my opinion, a layout with a width of 1,000 pixels is still a good choice for most of the cases. Such width ensures that the site will be displayed correctly on a pretty old, but still commonly used, nonwide 17" monitor. (The typical resolution for this hardware is 1,024 x 768 and such a layout will fill the whole screen.) As more and more users have now started using computers that are equipped with a far better screen, you can consider increasing the resolution slightly, to, for example, 1,150 pixels. Remember that not every user will visit your site using a desktop. Many laptops, and especially netbooks and tablets, don't have wide screens either.

Remember that the width of the page must be a little lower than the total resolution of the screen. You should reserve some space for the vertical scrollbar.

We are going to set up the width of our project traditionally to 1,000 pixels. To do this, click on the **Layout** tab on the ribbon, and next to the **Sheet Width** button. Choose **1000 pixels** from the available options on the list.

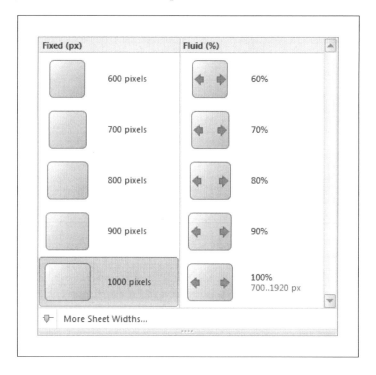

The **Sheet Options** window is divided into two areas: on the left you can choose from the values expressed in pixels, while on the right, as a percentage. The percentage value means that the page doesn't have a fixed width, but it will change according to the parameters of the screen it is displayed on (according to the chosen percentage value). Designing layouts with the width defined in percentage might seem to be a great idea; and indeed, this technique, when properly used, can lead to great results. But you have to remember, that in such a case, all page elements have to be similarly prepared in order, to be able to adapt to the dynamically changing width of the site. It is far simpler to achieve good results for the layout with fixed values (expressed in pixels).

It is a common rule while working with Artisteer that after clicking on a button on the ribbon, you get the list containing the most commonly used standard values. If you need a custom value, however, you can click on the button located at the bottom of the list to go to a window where you can freely set up and choose the required value. For example, while choosing the width of a layout, clicking on the **More Sheet Widths...** button (located just under the list) will lead you to a window where you can set up the required width with an accuracy up to 1 pixel.

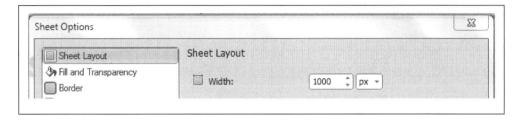

We can set the required value in three ways:

- We can click on the up and down arrows that are located on the right side of the field.

- We can move the mouse cursor on the field and use the slider that appears.

- We can click on the field. The text cursor will appear. Then we can type the required value using the keyboard. For me, this is the most comfortable way, especially since the slider's minimal progress is more than 1.

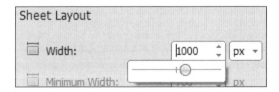

Panel mode versus windows mode

If you look carefully at the displayed windows, on the bottom-right corner you will see a panel mode button. This button switches Artisteer's interface between panel mode and windows mode. In the windows mode, the advanced settings are displayed in windows. In the panel mode, the advanced settings are displayed on the side panel located on the right side of Artisteer's window. If you are using a wide screen, you may find the panel mode to be more comfortable. Its advantage is that the side panel doesn't cover anything on your project, so you have a better view to observe the changes. Such a change is persistent and if you switch to the panel mode, all the advanced settings will be displayed in the right panel, as long as you decide to go back into the windows mode. To reverse, find and click on the icon located in the top-right corner of the side panel (just next to the **x** button that closes the panel).

Columns and their content

The next step while designing a template with Artisteer is usually to decide how many columns should the layout contain. In our project, we are going to use the two-column layout, with the bigger column for the content and the other, narrower one, on the left. In this column, we want to display a vertical menu and put a block with the contact information. These two elements will be displayed on all pages.

When you add a special block to your project, it is displayed on every page. Unfortunately you can't exclude a block from being displayed on specific pages. That's why we have to choose the blocks whose display on every page makes sense.

Fortunately, this limitation has no importance when you're designing for CMS.

We are beginning with setting up the number of columns. Click on the **Columns** button in the **Layout** tab on the ribbon. From the available options, choose the one with two columns, with the narrower one on the left.

Now have a look at the content of the left column. There is a vertical menu with a search block. We wanted a vertical menu there, but we didn't plan for a search block. We have to delete this block and replace it with one presenting our contact information. Perform the following steps:

1. Move the mouse pointer over the search block. According to the location of the pointer, Artisteer will highlight various elements inside the block. Place the mouse pointer a little below the block's title to make the program frame the whole block.

2. In the top-right corner of the block, you will find two icons. The first one, which looks like a bulb, is used to start **Suggestion Tool**, whose scope is limited to the elements inside the border. The second one, which looks like a list with a red cross, removes from the project all the elements inside the border. If you click on that icon, the whole block will disappear. You will have to confirm your decision in a confirmation dialog box that Artisteer displays to make sure you are not removing anything by mistake.

3. Click on the **New Block** button (we are still in the **Layout** tab). Artisteer will put a brand new block under the vertical menu:

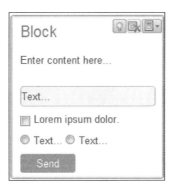

Now we have to change the title of our new block and write some content in it. Perform the following steps:

1. Click on the block's title (**New Block**) and delete the Block text using your keyboard. Then type the new title: Contact.

2. Click a little below (the border will show you the place) and type your own contact information: telephone number and email address.

When all the changes are done, your new block should look similar to the following:

The way we have changed the text inside our new block is the standard way for editing content in Artisteer. Up to Version 2.6 of the program, content editing was impossible. Starting from Version 3.0, you can freely edit the content on all pages of the project. Starting from Version 4.0, this is possible not only in HTML templates, but also when designing for CMS. The content can be exported along with the design and imported into the CMS.

Note that while you write the content, the ribbon automatically switches to the **Edit** tab, where you can find typical editorial functions. Here you can, for example, set the font, alignment, and insert pictures or tables. The symbols used to designate the various options are similar to those you find in any popular word processor—if you have experience with MS Word, this will be very intuitive.

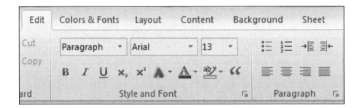

Colors

The default **Blank** project is in white. Before we start designing the various elements of our template, we are going to change the color theme, by choosing one of the available themes in blue. To do this, follow these steps:

1. Choose the **Colors & Fonts** tab on the ribbon.
2. Click on the **Color Themes** button.
3. Find the **Sky Blue** group on the list, and choose the **Depth** theme.

Perhaps you have already noticed that Artisteer dynamically shows you the results of the changes not only after you choose an option (that is, the color theme), but also while you move the mouse pointer over the various options.

Background

After we have chosen the color scheme, it's time to set up the background of our site. Choose the **Background** tab on the ribbon to see the available options.

At the beginning, we must decide whether our background should be a solid color, gradient, a texture, or maybe a picture. Some of these options are mutually exclusive, while some can coexist. The relationships between them are shown in the following diagram:

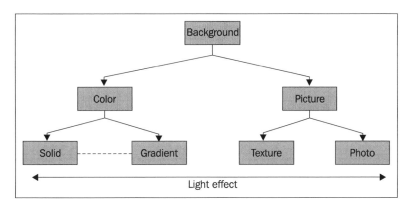

If you set up a color for your background, it doesn't exclude the use of a gradient. But the simultaneous use of a texture and picture is impossible. If you want your background to be a solid color or a gradient, you have to choose **No Texture** in the **Picture or Image** list. Otherwise, the chosen picture or texture will override the chosen color.

The last group of tools include **Light Effect**, which adds to your background a delicate effect that resembles a light glow. The options from the **Light Effect** group relate to both the colors and gradients, and the textures and pictures.

For our project, we are going to set up a color background with a gradient. Click on the **Fill Color** button, and from the **Theme Colors** list, choose the third color from the left in the second row. Then click on the **Gradient** button and in the **Light to Dark** group choose the first option from the left, in the second row:

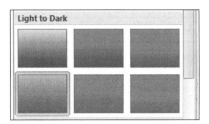

For the light effect, choose the first option in the **Classic** group.

Pages

We should now add the pages to our project according to the schema. We have to delete the pages that Artisteer has inserted by default and replace them with our set of pages, maintaining the relationship among them. You can manage the pages with the help of the side panel on the left side.

Adding, removing, and renaming the pages

In the first step we will remove the redundant pages. If you look at the **Pages** panel, you will see that the first page contains two subpages. But in our project (look at the schema again), the first page does not contain any subpages. We are going to remove these subpages, since we don't need them. Follow these steps:

1. Click on the small triangle symbol on the left of **Page 1** to expand its subpages (another way to do it is to just double-click on the page name).

2. Right-click on **Page 3** and from the context menu choose **Delete** (you can also select the page with a single left mouse click and pressing *Delete* on the keyboard).

3. Repeat this procedure for all subpages of **Page 1** to remove them.

 A single mouse click selects a page, but in case the clicked page was already selected, a single mouse click is used to rename it.

Now we are going to add the missing pages. Our project assumes four pages on the top level, so we need to add two more pages:

1. Right-click on **Page 2** and from the context menu choose **New Page**. Artisteer will add a new page and name it as **Page 3**. The name of this page will be highlighted to enable you to rename it.

2. Type Offer and press *Enter*.

   Similarly, add the **Contact** page and rename the first two pages by choosing from the **Rename** context menu. You should have following pages: **Home**, **About Me**, **Offer**, and **Contact**.

3. Right-click on the **Offer** page and from the context menu choose **New Child Page**. Name the new subpage as **Websites**. Analogically add the other missing subpages.

Page properties

OK, our project now contains all the pages we wanted. You can observe that all the pages are displayed as items in both our menus (the horizontal menu expands by hovering, while the vertical menu expands on clicking, by default). We have renamed the pages, but the names we have given them are not the names of the files that will be generated during the export process, but only the names that appear in the menu.

> The name of the page that you see in the **Pages** panel is the name shown in the menu. It is neither the name of the file that will be generated, nor the page title that will be shown in the browser. These parameters have to be defined in the **Properties** window. In this window, we can also define the menu in which the page should be displayed.

Let's define the properties for the **Home** page:

1. In the **Pages** panel, right-click on the **Home** page, and from the context menu choose **Properties**. It will display the **Properties** window.

2. Make sure that the **General** tab (from the list on the left side of the window) is active.

3. In the **Name/URL** field, type: index.

4. In the **Title** field, type: Welcome to my page.

5. Click on the **OK** button to close the window.

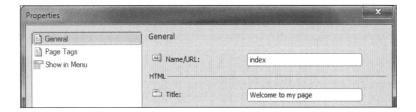

The **Name/URL** field defines the name of the file that will be generated during the export process, and this name appears in the browser's address bar. Because it's a filename it cannot contain characters that are forbidden in filenames (for example, "?"). Also, it cannot contain any spaces. If the desired name consists of two or more words, you can use the "-" character instead of a space (for example, for our **About Me** page, a good name would be: about-me). Remember that Linux is case-sensitive (in most cases, the server where you have your hosting account is powered by Linux), so to avoid any trouble, a good practice is to use only lowercase letters.

The **Title** field contains the title of the page that is displayed in the browser's window (and in the browser's tab). In this field, you can use any character you want. This title is also displayed by the search engines, such as Google, Bing, and Yahoo!. As you can see, it's an important property.

> For most web servers, the default file that is displayed when no specific file is specified is index.html or index.htm. That's why you should insert index in the **Name/URL** field for the main page of your website. Artisteer will generate this page as the index.html file. Thanks to this, your home page will be displayed by default when the visitor puts only your domain name into the browser's address bar (without specifying the concrete page).

Similarly, define these parameters for the rest of the pages in our project.

Header

Now that we have designed the overall layout, page width, and background, and added pages, it is time to design the various elements of our template. We are going to start with the header. First of all, we want it (the header) to be a little higher. Click on the **Header** tab on the ribbon and look for the **Height** button. Click on it and from the list of available options choose **150px**. The header will adopt the new size.

Next, we will define the header's background. Just like the background of the page, the header's background can be a solid color, a gradient, a texture, or a picture. Expand the **Background Image** list, and from the **Abstract** group choose the first option from the left in the second row.

Title and slogan

In Artisteer, the template's header contains two standard texts: **Title** and **Slogan**.

Title is just the title of your website presented in the header (do not confuse this text with the title you defined in the **Page Properties** window). Slogan is the second standard text in the header and usually contains a motto.

Title and slogan editing is done in the same way as editing the rest of the text in the page (remember how we edited the block with the contact information?). To edit the slogan and title, perform the following steps:

1. Double-click on the title **Enter Site Title**.

2. Using the keyboard, delete the existing text and type:
   `Stunning Web Design`.

3. Click on anything other than the header to apply the changes.

The title gets deactivated when you click on something else. If you click on it once, a delicate border will appear around it, and you will be able to freely move and rotate the text. Note that it's impossible to move the title outside the header.

 The previous technique of moving and rotating an object can be applied not only to the title, but also to the slogan and the shapes.

Now we will add the slogan to our header:

1. Click on the **Slogan** button on the ribbon. In the header's area a new text **Enter Site Slogan** will appear.

2. Delete the original text and replace it with `We design your needs` in the same way that we modified the title.

3. Place the slogan under the title.

Note that while editing the title and the slogan, the ribbon does not switch automatically to the **Edit** tab, and even if you do it manually, all the options located on the **Edit** tab are unavailable. Does it mean that you can't influence the appearance of these elements? Oh no! If you want to change the look of the title or slogan, you have to use the **Text** button that is located in the **Edit Shape** group, on the **Header** tab on the ribbon. This group of options is displayed only if the title or slogan is selected. Experiment with all the available options and make these two elements look exactly like you want.

Pictures

Besides the title and slogan you can insert images into the header. We are now going to insert a picture into the header:

1. Click on the lower part — the arrow — of the **Image** button. This button consists of two elements. Clicking on the upper part fires the **From File...** option, while clicking on the bottom arrow expands the full list of options.

2. Find the **Animals** group on the list.

3. Choose the picture of two colorful parrots.

You can freely move and resize the inserted picture with the mouse (while resizing, the Artisteer program maintains the aspect ratio of the picture). Note that while a picture is selected, a new group of options, **Edit Shape**, is displayed on the ribbon. It's at the same place where we found the **Edit Image** group, while we were editing the title and the slogan. This group contains the options by which you can align a picture, convert it to grayscale, or add the glow effect.

 You can put as many pictures as you want in the header.

Shapes

Shapes are graphic objects (in the form of geometric figures) that you can insert into the header. You can also move and rotate the shapes like you did with the title and the slogan, and you can resize them just like you did with the picture (even better because you can resize the shapes with or without maintaining the aspect ratio). You can also type text inside them by double-clicking on the shape and enabling the text cursor in it. The background of the shape can be a solid color, gradient, or texture.

Each shape can have one of the several predefined forms. The available forms contain simple geometric figures and also some more advanced shapes. The list of available forms is displayed after clicking on the **Shape** button on the ribbon:

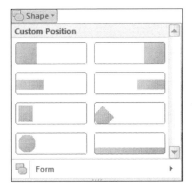

The last option on this list (**Form**) expands another list, with more advanced forms:

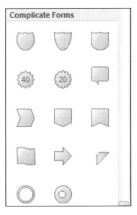

Using shapes can be very handy. They are especially useful when combined with images:

Example of the combination of a shape (on the left, with phone number) and an image

One of the most interesting features offered by shapes is the ability to use masks.

A **Mask** is the transparent area within the shape. Because shapes are always displayed over images, moving a shape with a mask over the image makes the image visible through the shape. The possibility of uncovering only a part of the image allows you to achieve interesting effects, as in the following screenshot:

Ordering shapes and pictures

If you use many pictures and shapes in your header, sooner or later you will come across the problem of deciding which one of them should be on top of the other and which one should be covered. In Artisteer, you can set the order of these objects by choosing the **Send to Back** or **Bring to Front** option from the context menu that appears when you right-click on the shape/image:

The order of the shapes and images should be considered separately. You can display one picture over/under another picture, or display one shape over/under another shape. But you can't display a picture over any shape. The shapes are always displayed over the pictures.

Flash

If you want, you can add one of the available Flash effects to the header. To do this, click on the **Flash** button (it's on the right side of the ribbon, on the **Header** tab) and choose one of the effects from the list (I chose the second effect from the **Special** group). You can also insert your own Flash movie (in the swf format) from the disc.

The characteristic feature of the Flash effects that Artisteer offers out-of-the-box is that they don't replace the content of the header, but display the rather delicate additional effects over it.

Although adding Flash to the header can make it look more attractive, you should remember that Flash is not natively supported on the devices working under iOS, such as iPad or iPhone. If you expect visitors to browse your site using one of these devices, using Flash is not the best option.

Menu

The next elements we are going to design are our menus. We will style their look and also decide which pages they should display as their items.

Horizontal menu

All the options that Artisteer provides to design the horizontal menu are located on the **Menu** tab on the ribbon. Click on it.

Currently our horizontal menu is located inside the header and is aligned to the right. Because this place is now occupied by an image, the menu isn't clearly visible. The first thing we are going to do is find a better place for our menu. We will put it under the header and align it to the left.

The position of the vertical menu is determined by the **Position** option, located as the second icon from the left, next to **Suggest Menu**. Expand the available positions and see how the position of the menu changes according to each one. For our project, choose the second position in the **Inside Sheet** group. The menu will move under the header.

If you want to have some space between the menu and the header, use the **Margin** option. The **Length** option lets you set the menu's width to be equal to the header or as wide as the whole screen.

Our next step is the alignment of menu items to the left. It's a little bit tricky because the correct option is located not inside the **Menu Area** group, but in **Item**. (I must admit it's logical, since you don't align the menu area but the menu items. On the other hand you can't align a single item, but all of them at once. Anyway, it took me some time to find this option when I started my adventure with Artisteer.) To change the alignment of the menu, do the following:

1. Click on the **Item** button.
2. On the list, find the **Layout** group and expand the **Align** option by moving the mouse pointer over it.

3. From the available options choose the icon that represents alignment to the left:

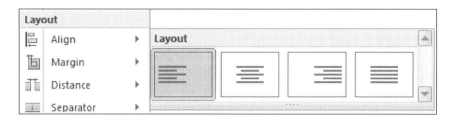

If you want to quickly change the look of the whole menu, use one of the options available in the **Menu Styles** list. Each one of the options listed there changes the look of the whole menu, including all of its elements. If you want to define each menu element separately, you should use the options available in the **Menu** and **Submenu** groups.

The **Menu** group contains options to modify the top level of the menu. The group is divided into four main options, each of which has its own, more detailed properties.

Menu Area

Menu Area is a container (rectangular area) in which the menu is displayed. It doesn't define the look of the menu items. The items are located inside the menu area. In other words, the menu area is just the menu bar.

Item

With the help of this option you can define the look of the top-level items in the menu.

Coloring

This option lets you set up the style in which the active item is marked.

The last three options (**Active**, **Passive**, and **Hovered**) let you precisely design the look of menu items according to the three states that they can be in:

- **Active menu item**: It's an item that represents the page currently being displayed. It's a good idea to make the active item look different than the others, because it allows the visitor to quickly find out which page he is currently viewing.

- **Passive menu item**: It's an item that is neither active nor hovered.

- **Hovered menu item**: It's an item under your mouse pointer. Featuring an item using mouseover is commonly used for a decorative effect.

You may wonder, what is the sense of using the **Item** option, and when will you design the look of the items separately for each of their three states? Well, I must say that you have a point. The options you find in the **Item** list have more of a general character and apply to all the menu items at once (please note, that they don't give you the possibility to choose something basic such as color). In case the basic setting from **Item** interferes with the settings defined for a particular state (active, passive, or hover), then the priority has the more detailed settings.

The **Submenu** group contains the options that are analogous to those from the **Menu** group, except that they apply not to the top-level items, but to subitems. This group has **Passive** and **Hover**, but there's no **Active** here—and this is not a mistake. The horizontal menu expands by mouseover, and when the mouse pointer is moved out it collapses, and is shown again only to the top-level items. So the active subitem is never visible, it is always collapsed. That's why the subitems are never in the active state.

Levels

Have a look at the first button called **Items** in the **Submenu** group. This is the one of the most important buttons in the **Menu** tab. It defines the look and feel of the whole menu. Click on it, and you will see a list of the following five options:

- **No submenu (no subitems)**
- **One column**
    - **Multilevel**
    - **Extended**
- **Multi-column**
    - **Megamenu**
    - **Megamenu extended**

To better understand the meaning of these variants, let's consider a site with the following structure:

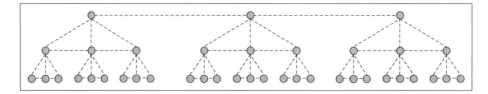

We have three items on the top level. Each of these items has three of its own subitems, and each of those subitems also has three of its own subitems. Let's see how each variant of the the horizontal menu will look for a site with the structure as presented in the previous diagram.

No submenu (no subitems)

This is the first and most basic variant of the horizontal menu. In this variant, the horizontal menu displays only the top-level items. Subitems aren't displayed at all:

One column – multilevel

In this variant, our menu shows the top-level items and also the subitems. The subitems are presented in a column, just below the parent top-level item. The next level items are presented in the column on the right (or on the left if the parent item is displayed on the right edge of the screen). This menu resembles the standard menu of the classic desktop applications:

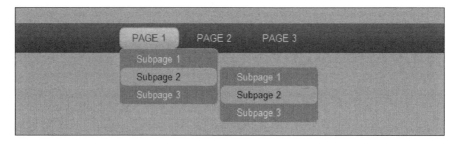

One column – extended

This kind of menu is very similar to the one described in the previous section. The only difference is how the top-level item is marked when expanding. While in the previous example the column containing subitems was separated from its parent (top-level item), in this case they together make a simple unit:

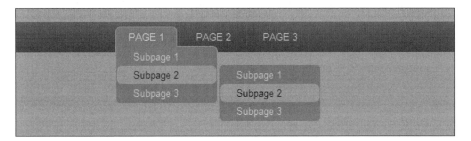

Multi-column – megamenu

This kind of menu (introduced in Artisteer 4) presents the subitems in many columns. The second-level items are displayed in a row (they are in bold), and the third-level items are displayed below in the form of columns. If the menu includes further levels, they are displayed just like in the previous variants (new column to the right of the parent item):

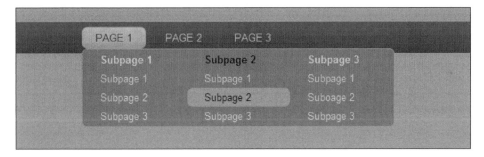

Multi-column – megamenu extended

The difference between **Megamenu** and **Megamenu Extended** is analogous to the difference between **Multilevel** and **Extended** in one-column styles. **Megamenu Extended** is **Megamenu** with those difference, that is, the top-level item is joined with subitems.

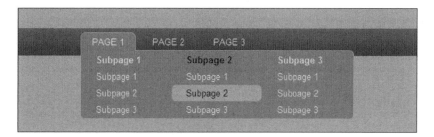

For our project, we will choose **One-column | Multilevel**.

We will also define the look of our menu, but instead of designing every aspect individually, we will use the **Menu Styles** option. Click on the button and choose the first option in the fifth row. Our template should currently look like this:

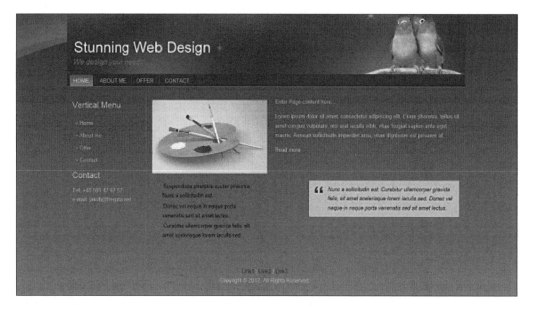

Vertical menu

Even if you are satisfied with our horizontal menu, we can't forget about our vertical menu. Click on the **Vertical Menu** tab on the ribbon and we can start.

The available options located in the **Vertical Menu** tab are ordered similar to the those on the **Menu** tab. First on the left (as always) we have **Suggestion Tool**, followed by the **Layout** group (don't confuse it with the **Layout** tab!), which contains only one button (it's rather a small group, isn't it?). This is an important button, which determines the location of the vertical menu. Let's click on it.

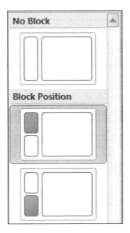

This list that is displayed is divided into two groups: **No block** and **Block Position**. The second group contains several options that change the location of the vertical menu. The target position is marked as filled area on the icon. Switch among the options and observe that the vertical menu is moving from one position to another. Note that you don't have to necessarily display the vertical menu in a side column, although in most cases displaying the vertical menu above or below the content is not the best idea.

The content of this list changes according to the layout of the project. Had we chosen a three-column layout for example, you would see many more options in it.

The first group (**No Block**) contains only one icon. By enabling this option you decide not to display the vertical menu at all.

Choosing the **No Block** option is the same as if you delete the vertical menu using the icon located on its top-right corner (remember how we removed the search block?). If you remove the vertical menu, you can restore it to the project at any time by choosing any other position in the **Position** list.

The **Styles** button works analogically to the **Menu Styles** button from the **Menu** tab. It lets you define the look of the whole menu very quickly, by choosing one of predefined options. Similarly, the options from the **Menu Area**, **Item**, and **Submenu** groups work analogically to their equivalents, which we used while designing the horizontal menu. As they are very similar, we won't describe them one by one, but rather focus on the differences between the vertical and horizontal menus (of course, the main difference is that one is vertical, and the other horizontal).

The vertical menu is actually a kind of block (anything displayed in the side column is a block). Like any other block, the vertical menu may or may not have a header (title text). You can hide (or show, if it's already hidden) this header, and also choose one of the predefined styles of the vertical menu with the list of options on the **Menu Block** button. Note that there is no other way to remove the header. You can edit and change its text, but even if you remove all the characters, you will still have a header (although an empty one). You also cannot remove the header from a block using the icon in the top-right corner. Even if the border or frame encloses only the header and not the whole block, clicking on the icon removes the whole block.

The horizontal menu always expands on mouseover and collapses automatically. The vertical menu may behave differently, depending on the settings. The active subitems may be visible, so it makes sense to design the look for all the three states (active, passive, and hovered). That's why **Active**, **Passive**, and **Hovered** buttons are present for both the items and subitems of the vertical menu.

Vertical menu behavior

The possible options for defining the vertical menu behavior are available with the **Levels** button, which is located in the **Submenu** group.

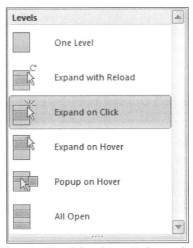

Available styles that define the vertical menu behavior

We can choose from six kinds of vertical menu behavior:

- **One Level** is the most basic kind of menu that you can choose. It displays only the top-level items. No subitems are displayed at all.

- The **Expand with Reload** menu shows both items and subitems. The items containing subitems expand on a mouse click. After the click, the page is reloaded.

- The **Expand on Click** menu is very similar to **Expand with Reload** with the difference that the items expand without reloading.

 You may think that **Expand on Click** is better than **Expand with Reload** (it looks the same, but without the need of reloading the page). But the most important difference is not about reloading. Rather, it is that in **Expand with Reload**, the item containing subitems is a link to the page, while in **Expand on Click** it's only the menu item without any corresponding page. Consider our project: we have an **Offer** page that contains three subpages. Set the vertical menu as **Expand on Click** and export the page, then open the exported folder and click twice on the `index.html` file. The page will open in your system's default browser. Click on the **Offer** item in the vertical menu. The page is reloaded and you may see that the **Offer** page is displayed (look at the address bar of your browser, where you will see `offer.html` at the end of the address). Then go back to Artisteer, change the vertical menu, type `Expand on Click`, export the page, and run again. You will see that when you click on the **Offer** item in the vertical menu, the menu expands, but you can't access the **Offer** page at all.

I don't mean to tell you that **Expand on Click** is bad. There certainly are projects where it will be far better than **Expand with Reload** and vice versa.

- In the **Expand on Hover** menu, the item containing subitems expands on hover, without the need to click. The parent item is still a link to a page.

- The **Popup on Hover** menu expands on hover, just like a horizontal menu, but vertically.

Example of Expands on Hover vertical menu in action

- The **All Open** menu always displays all of its subitems (it is never collapsed).

We are going to design the look of our menu very quickly using one of the available options in **Styles**. Click on the **Styles** button, and from the list choose the second option in the second row. We would also like to hide the header of this menu. Click on the **Menu Block** button, and from the **Simple** group choose the second option. As the menu type, choose **All Open** by clicking on the last option from the list on the **Level** button. The last thing we want to change is the radius of an item. Click on the **Item** button (in the **Menu** group), expand the **Radius** option, and choose **10% of Height**.

Determining the pages displayed in menus

In both the **Menu** and **Vertical Menu** tabs on the ribbon you can find the **Pages** group containing only one button, **Show in Menu**. Clicking on this button displays the **Select pages in menu** window in which you can decide which pages should be displayed in the menu, and which should not. We want all the pages to be displayed in the horizontal menu, and only the **Offer** page (with all of its subpages) to be displayed in the vertical menu. Check the appropriate pages.

For vertical menu we want to display only Offer page with its subpages

Note that you cannot check the subpages without checking their parent page too (or more precisely, you can; but if you do that, they won't be displayed although you have checked them). That's why we have to not only check the **Websites**, **WordPress**, **Joomla!**, and **DotNetNuke** pages, but also their parent page **Offer**.

By now, your vertical menu should look like the following screenshot:

We have designed the look and feel of the horizontal and vertical menus and have also set up the pages to be displayed in each of them. Our next step will be designing the content area.

Content

Before we start writing our content, we must design the overall layout of our content. In Artisteer, the content area can be divided into any number of rows and columns. Skilful identification of rows and columns is the key to achieve well-designed content.

The first thing to plan is the look of the site. We are going to design the main site with following content:

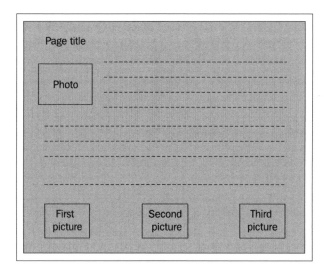

At the top of the content we want to have the title. In the large area below it we want to have a description about who we are and what we do (remember that we are creating a site advertising you as a web designer). We want to enrich the text with a photo. Below it we want just a one row of text: `Look at our latest projects...`. The last area will contain three pictures with a thumbnail of your latest projects. If you haven't done any projects yet, don't worry! Design something quickly using the Auto Suggestion tool and customize it using the information you have read up till now. Actually, it will be a good exercise to get some practice with the program. If you feel you can't do that yet, you can just insert any pictures from Artisteer's library here and replace them later.

In our case, the combination of rows and cells should be similar to the following picture (for better clarity, the rows and cells are bordered):

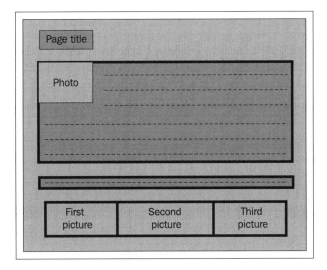

We need three rows for our content. The first row is for the biggest section of text (description), the second is for the short text below it, and the last row — divided into three cells — to is for inserting three logos.

You may wonder why we don't create a row for the page title. It's because Artisteer creates the container for the title automatically. It's a similar situation to that of the vertical menu header. You can hide the page title, but you cannot design any page without it. We will learn how to hide the page title a little later in this chapter.

You may wonder why the first photo isn't placed into a separate cell while the next three logos are. It's because the photo in the first row is not a separate element of our content. The first row contains an article, and the photo is a part of it.

Before we can set up the layout for our content, we have to remove the actual content that the program put here automatically. And to do that efficiently, we have to know the tools that Artisteer offers for creating the content layout.

All of the tools to design the content layout are located in the **Content** pane on the ribbon. Click on it. There are not too many options. But when you click anywhere in the content area, the number of tools (displayed in the **Content** pane) increases and many new buttons appear. You will see that many new buttons appear.

 Artisteer shows the full range of content-designing tools only when you're editing the content.

The tools applied to the layout design are located in the **Content** group.

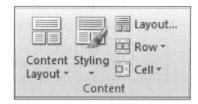

The first button, **Content Layout**, displays a list of the most used content layouts. You may think of it as a kind of template that you can assign to your page with just one mouse click. Choosing one of the available options will replace your current layout with the chosen one, and all of your content will be automatically updated to the new structure of rows and cells.

The second button, **Styling**, lets you style your content. While in the previous list you could define the layout, this is the place where you can define how it looks. The **Styling** options define various borders and backgrounds for your rows and cells.

 The options displayed in the **Styling** list depend on the layout you chose in **Content Layout**.

The last option in the **Styling** list lets you define the layout for your current row and also defines some settings that apply to all pages, such as the border of the cells, margins, and radius.

We have to remove the current content. We could, of course, click on every row and cell and remove the text one by one, but we will make it faster and a little tricky. If you change the layout, the content is preserved and automatically adopted to the new layout. So, we can use this feature to delete all the content at once. Perform the following steps:

1. Click on the **Content Layout** button.

2. From the list, choose the only available option in the **One Column** group. The current content layout will be replaced with only one row, which will contain all the content.

3. Click anywhere within the content and press *Ctrl + A*. All the content will be selected.

4. Press *Delete* to remove the current content.

Now we can start designing our layout. Because there's no such layout on the **Content Layout** list, we will design it manually. Click on the **Layout...** button to display the **Layout Editor** window:

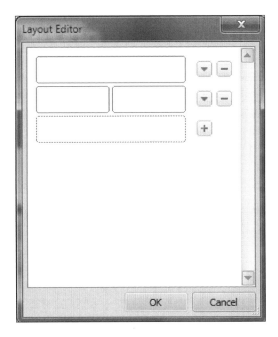

In the previous window you can almost freely design your own layout. The frames on the left side represent the rows and cells. The first button to the right (in the shape of an inverted triangle) allows you to change the style of the row (the number and proportion of the cells) by displaying a list with the available options. The second button (the red minus sign) removes the whole row.

 You can delete the whole row, with all its columns, but you can't delete a single cell.

We are going to modify the layout from scratch. Do the following:

1. Delete all the rows using the buttons with the red minus sign. Actually we could just modify the existing rows, but we want to design it from scratch.

2. Add a new row by clicking on the button with the green plus sign, and from the list of the available row variations choose the first option — the row that is not divided into more cells. We want to have the article with photo in this first row.

3. Add a second row to the content layout. This one will contain our `Look at our latest projects...` statement. This is also a single-cell row.

4. Add the third and last row. This row will contain our three thumbnail pictures. Because they will be put as separate elements (and not inserted into the article), we need to have three cells in this row. Choose and click on the correct option.

5. Click on **OK** to close this window. Apparently nothing has happened. But if you move your mouse cursor over the content area, you will see the borders appearing on the new areas. Thus, Artisteer has indeed modified the layout.

Writing articles

Now that we have defined the areas in our content layout, we can start filling our site with content.

We will first change the title. Right-click on the **Home** page on the left panel, and from the context menu choose **Show Article Title**:

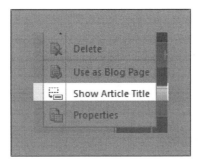

The title will be shown above the first row in the content area. We haven't edited it yet so it still contains the text **Page 1**. Click on the title and change it to `Welcome to my site!`.

Now we are going to write our article. It wouldn't be very useful to write all the articles in the book. Instead of this, we will copy and paste some dummy text.

This is a common practice that when designing a layout, you fill it with sample text. Without this the end customer won't know how the template will look as a live website. It also allows you to design and present the typography. There is a common standard for a sample text—lorem ipsum.

To get dummy text just go to `http://www.lipsum.com` and find the **Generate Lorem Ipsum** button. Change the number of generated paragraphs to three and click on it. Then copy the generated text to the clipboard and return to Artisteer. In Artisteer, click on the first row in your content area and press *Ctrl + V* to paste the text. From the **Paragraph** group on the ribbon click on the icon that will justify the text:

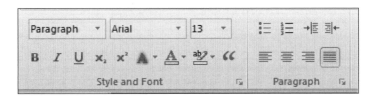

You can type the text just like in any text editor. If you would like to change the font or start a list, all the tools you need are located in the **Style and Font** and **Paragraph** groups.

While writing the content you should remember one particular rule: if you need to change the font (that is, you want to write a header), you should use the styles instead of manipulating the font property directly. Thanks to this, your content will look consistent throughout the site. Remember that all the typography, including six levels of headers, links, and button texts is defined with your layout. On a regular basis, there's hardly ever a need to use something other than the defined styles.

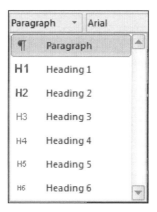

Inserting images

We have our first row filled with text, so now it's time to enrich the article with a picture. We want the picture be placed at the beginning of the article. To achieve this, do the following:

1. Click on the beginning of the article. The text cursor will blink right before the first word in the article.

2. Click on the triangle under the **Image** button (it's in the **Insert** group on the ribbon) and from the available options choose **Clip Art**. Another list presenting thumbnails of the pictures provided by Artisteer will expand.

3. Choose the fourth image in the second row.

The image is inserted, but not exactly as we expected. Firstly, it's far too large. Secondly, we would like the text to flow around the picture, and what we have is the picture with an empty space on the right!

Don't worry! We are going to correct this. Right-click on the image and from the context menu choose **Image Options...**. The **Image Options** window will appear. This window has three tabs on the left: **Image**, **Layout**, and **Link**. Make sure that the first tab is selected. Do the following:

1. Set the width of the picture to 150 px. The values in the **Height** and **Scale** fields will change automatically.

2. In the **Alt Text** field, type My photo (remember that we are designing your site, so you can exchange this picture with your real photo).

3. Click on the **Layout** tab on the left.

4. From the **Position** combobox choose **left**. Also, set the bottom margin to 0 px and the border to 2 px. Click on **OK** to close the window.

After the changes your site should look like this:

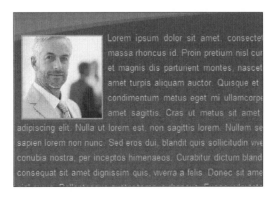

You should never leave the **Alt Text** field empty. **Alt Text** is the text that will be displayed when it's impossible to display the picture. For example, people with disabilities, who use a screen reader, will get only the alt text. Putting an image without any alt text may also cause problems with site validation.

There is another important feature that we have to discuss when talking about inserting images. By default, when an image is clicked, the bigger, overlaid version of this image is displayed on top of your page. This effect is called **Lightbox Style** (the name comes from the famous JavaScript library that had introduced this effect). It's perfect for creating image galleries, but sometimes you don't want the picture to behave like that.

To check whether the picture should have the Lightbox effect or not, you have to change the **Preview** settings in the **Image Options** window. It is the last option in the **Image** tab and contains two options: **Yes** and **No**. Set this value to **No** to turn off this effect for the image.

To finish our first page, we have to complete the content in the rest of our cells.

Click on the row below, and from the **Style and Font** group choose **Header 2** as the style (we want this text to be larger than the default text in the paragraphs). Type Look at my latest project..., click on the first cell in the third row, and click on the **Image** button. An **Open** dialog will appear. Select the file with a screenshot of any other project that you did in Artisteer (if you didn't, you can select any other image from your disk). Similarly, insert images into the last two cells. This time we won't turn off the Lightbox effect, because it's good that the visitor can click and enlarge these thumbnails.

If you preview this site in a browser, you will see that the Lightbox effect not only displays the larger image, but also the navigation buttons to the next and the previous images. This way we have created a gallery.

In the end, our site should look like this:

Inserting a slideshow

Besides inserting images and image galleries (with the Lightbox effect), Artisteer also offers the possibility of creating slideshows. A **slideshow** is a set of images, displayed one by one, at the same place. The slides that are shown change according to one of the predefined transition effects. You can create a slideshow in the content area and in the header.

Slideshow in the content area

We start preparing a slideshow by inserting a single image. This image will be the first slide to show, and it sets the dimensions of the overall slideshow. Every slide has the same size, so it's good practice to prepare the set of images and resize them accordingly before you start preparing the slideshow. You can insert several images into one slide, making a collage, or even combine pictures with shapes.

After you have inserted an image, click on it once with a left mouse click. The ribbon will show the **Edit** tab, and the **New Slide** button in the **Slideshow** group will be enabled. Click to insert a new slide from one of the available sources: you can insert a blank slide, duplicate the current slide, add an image from a file, add an image from Artisteer's library, or add an image from Flickr:

If you decide to insert a new slide from a file, you will also have the possibility to resize the image. The available options are:

- **Resize collage to image**: This option resizes the whole slideshow according to the dimensions of the new picture. Works only for those images that are smaller than the slideshow.

- **Resize image to collage**: This option adjusts the size of the inserted picture to fit the actual slideshow dimensions.

- **Use original size**: This option doesn't change the size of the inserted image. If the image is larger than the slideshow, only a part of the image will be displayed. If the image is smaller than the slideshow, it will be surrounded with a background.

You can also insert new images and shapes into an existing slide. To do that, use the **Add Image** or **Add Shape** buttons, which are located on the right side of the **New Slide** button that we used to insert a new slide. They work in a very similar fashion, but instead of inserting a new image (or shape) as a new slide, they just add it into the current one. You can create interesting effects by combining several images and shapes in one slide.

Two images and a shape combined into one slide

The **Background** button lets you choose a background for the slide. The background will be visible if the displayed picture (or pictures) is smaller than the dimensions of the slide. You can set up a different background for each slide.

The last three buttons in the **Slideshow** group are: **Play**, **Motion**, and **Navigator**.

- The **Play** button starts the slideshow and lets you see how it will look on the live site.

- The **Motion** button lets you choose one of the available transition effects. By default, the slides change with a fade effect. You can also set up the speed of the transition effect, the delay (for how long each slide is displayed), and whether the slideshow will be repeated or not.

- The **Navigator** button lets you design the navigator. A navigator is a group of pointers displayed in the bottom-right corner of the slideshow by default. It indicates which slide is currently displayed and lets you click and go to another one:

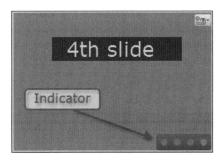

Slideshow in header

Creating a slideshow in the header is very similar to the process of placing a slideshow in the content. The difference is that you can have only one slideshow, and every slide covers the whole header. In fact, it's not a *slideshow in the header*, but rather *a slideshow of headers*.

In the **Header** pane on the ribbon, you will find the **Slide Show** group with buttons analogous to those we saw before in the **Edit** pane.

To create a slideshow, design your header as usual. Set up the background and insert images and shapes. This header will be the first slide. When everything is ready, click on the **New Slide** button and choose the image. A new slide (new header) will be inserted, and the chosen image will become its background. Design the header once again, and this will be the second slide, and so on.

 Think of every slide as a separate header, with its own background, images, and shapes. The only elements that are common to all slides are the headline, slogan, and a search field.

Typography

We have talked a little about typography. You know that you can use the styles instead of changing fonts for every header, and that the typography contains definitions for links, button text, and so on.

Now we will take a closer look into this template's parameters.

The typography tools are located on the **Colors & Fonts** tab on the ribbon. Click on it. As the name suggests, this tab contains the tools for typography and for working with template colors. The typography tools are placed on the **Fonts** group (beside **Suggestion Tool**). On this group you can find three buttons: **Font Sets**, **Typography**, and **Font Scale**.

The **Font Sets** button lets you choose the set of fonts to be used in your project. Every set consists of two fonts: the first font is the one that is used for headers, and the second is the font used for paragraph text. When you click on this button, you will see the list with the available font sets. Every list item displays the name of the font set, and also the names of the fonts used. The names of the fonts used are displayed with those fonts, giving you a preview of how they look.

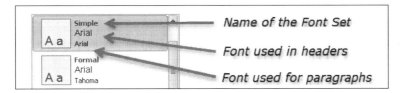

At the bottom of this list there's a button called **Edit Font Set**. Clicking on this button displays the **Edit Font Set** window, in which you can change the fonts used in the active state.

Let's pretend that we want the heading to be written in Arial, and the paragraphs in Times New Roman. We have to:

1. Display the **Edit Font Set** window.
2. Choose **Arial** in the **Heading Font** field.
3. Choose **Tahoma** in the **Text Font** field.
4. Click on the **OK** button to close the window.

Artisteer has changed the font, and if we click on the **Font Sets** button again, we will see that our set is now displayed in the **Custom** group as **Unsaved**. Indeed, this is our custom set, and we haven't saved it yet. Click on the **Save Font Set** button at the bottom (now that it's active) and save the file with the name My favorite fonts. Our new set will be displayed in the **Custom** group.

The font we have saved is not stored with only our template, it's stored in Artisteer on the application level. You can restart the program, open any other layout, or start creating a new one, and you will see that our **My favorite fonts** font set is available. This way the sets that you prepare can be reused in your future projects.

But typography is far more complex than the definition of font for headers and paragraphs. We have six levels of header, so it is obvious that there should be a possibility to define more properties. To edit the advanced features of typography, click on the **Typography** button. The list that will expand contains the available typographies. The active one is probably **Unsaved** on the **Custom** group.

Click on the **Edit Typography...** button at the bottom of the list to show the **Typography** window. In this window you can see all the text elements of the template. Below the list there's a **Modify** button, a **Preview** field where you can see how the selected element looks, and the element's CSS definition:

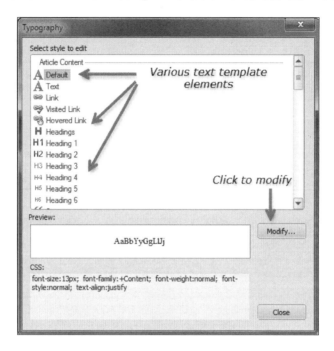

We will do the following modifications to our typography:

- We will modify the **Heading 6** element
- We will change the style of our text "Look at my latest projects..." from **Heading 2** to **Heading 6**. As a result, the look of our text should change.

To make these changes, do the following:

1. Click on the **Heading 6** element on the list to select it.

2. Click on the **Modify** button. A new window will appear.

3. In the **Font** tab of this window, set the font name as **Aguafina Script**, choose **Bold** as font style, and choose **28** as **Font Size**.

4. Click on the **OK** button to return to the previous window. Again, click on the **OK** button to close the window.

5. Click on our text. You don't have to select the entire text, it's enough if the text cursor blinks somewhere within the text.

6. The **Edit** tab of the ribbon should be automatically selected. Expand the list with the styles (you can find it in the **Style and Font** group) and choose **Heading 6**. The style of our text will change and look as we have designed.

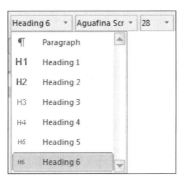

 We have changed the definition of the **Heading 6** element and applied it to `Look at my latest projects...` text. In our case this is acceptable, because we don't use the full typography in our project. If the structure of the content of our site is so complicated that we need all six heading levels, we cannot waste the header style for just text. Instead, we should set the text with the **Paragraph** style and then change the font manually. The overall rule for designing the header levels is that every next level should be a little smaller than the previous one, to visually illustrate the logical hierarchy of headers.

We are going to modify the paragraph text and make it a little larger, in the same way that we have changed the **Header 6** element. Similar to the **Header 6** element, edit the typography again, and in the **Typography** window, set the font size of the **Default** element to **14** px.

You can similarly modify any element of typography. Creating a good typography is not a trivial task, but an important factor of the overall template.

If you want to use our modified typography in the future, you can save it by any name using the **Save Typography** button.

The last button in the **Fonts** group is **Font Scale**. Using this button lets you change the size of all the text elements very quickly, all at once. The **Options...** button leads you to the window, where you can set the scale of text manually.

Color theme

We have chosen the color theme for our template, but we didn't go deeper into this topic. This was because we wanted to start with designing quickly, and also because we needed to know more about using Artisteer before we could take care of this problem.

Color theme is a set of colors used in a template. Logically it is similar to font sets and typography. Typography defines the text used in various template elements while a color theme defines their color.

To modify the color of the theme you can use the three buttons located in the **Paints** group (we are still in the **Fonts & Colors** tab). These three buttons, in the form of rectangles filled with a particular color, let you choose the color for paints.

Paints are the main colors used in a color theme. You may think of them as the basis on which the whole color theme is built. Every color theme in Artisteer has three paints.

There's no fixed relationship between a particular paint and a template element. You cannot say, for example, that changing the second paint will always change the color of the background. The distribution of theme colors will change in various templates.

With the last button, having the label **Adjust**, you can change the brightness and saturation of all paints in the color theme. The available options are divided into four groups, whose names suggest the changes (Basic, Normal, Contrast, and Pastel).

If you have modified the paints in a color theme and you are happy with the changes, you can save it under any name, and use it in your future projects.

Footer

The last thing we need to design is the footer. All the tools that apply to the footer are located on the **Footer** tab—although, you will see that's not so evident in this case. The problem is that many of the things you can define with the tools from the **Footer** tab, you can also achieve using the analogous tools from the **Edit** tab. What's more, the settings made by the tools from the **Edit** tab have a higher priority than the settings made from the tools located in the **Footer** tab. For example, you can align the footer text to the right using the **Align** button in the **Footer** tab, and at the same time align the same text to the left, using the align icon from the **Edit** tab. As a result, the text will be aligned to the left.

If the settings from the **Footer** tab are in conflict with the settings from the **Edit** tab, the settings from the **Edit** tab have a higher priority.

If you feel that the options in the **Footer** tab are not working at all, check if you have set the same property that with use of tool located in the **Edit** tab. For example, if you have set the color of the text in the **Edit** tab, changing it with the button in the **Footer** tabwon't have any effect because this property is covered by the setting with a higher priority, coming from the **Edit** tab tool.

The tools on the **Footer** tab are divided into two groups: **Layout** and **Footer Styles**. The first button in the **Layout** group, **Length and Position**, lets you choose one of the three types of footers. (To have a better understanding of how they work, you can temporarily set a different background color for the whole footer using the **Fill** button.)

The **Inside Sheet** footer is located inside your template. There's some site background on the left, on the right, and under the footer:

Inside Sheet footer: there's some background below and on both sides of the footer

The **Sheet Width, Screen Height** footer fills the whole space up to the bottom of the screen. There is no empty space (background) under the footer:

Sheet Width, Screen Height footer: the footer fills all the space below

The **Page Width, Screen Height** footer fills all the space under the content, and it's as wide as the whole page. There are no empty spaces (background) on the left, on the right, and below the footer:

Page Width, Screen Height footer: the footer fills all the places under the content

The **Margin** button lets you define the vertical space between the bottom edge of the content and the top edge of the footer.

For our project, choose the **Inside Sheet** option.

With the **Fill** button you can define the color of the footer pane. The list of available colors presents the colors belonging to the color theme. You can also click on **More Colors...** and freely choose from the full palette. The last button on this list lets you set up the transparency of the footer pane.

For our project, choose the first color from the second row (from the **Theme Colors** group) and set the transparency to 50 percent.

The **Separator** button lets you define the look of the line that separates the footer. You can set the width (**Weight**), the style, and the color of this line.

You shouldn't have any problem with the rest of the buttons, since they behave like analogical tools placed on the other tabs. The only surprise waiting for you is when you click on the **Text** button. Click on it and you will be redirected to the **Edit** tab on the ribbon bar!

Summary

We went through the whole process of creating a simple website. We have designed its structure and added proper subpages to our project. You then learned what the main elements of a typical template are and how to design them using Artisteer. We did it one by one, from the header to the footer. At this moment you have a complete project of your first site:

The subpages are without content as of yet, but the design is ready. The menus work correctly, and the images at the bottom use the Lightbox effect. You can now export this project as an HTML website (as we did in *Chapter 1, Meet the Artisteer*) or if you plan for this site to grow, export it as a package that is ready-to-use with one of the supported CMSs. This is what we will cover in the next chapter.

3
CMS Templates

Until this moment, we have focused on designing static websites (it's called an Website Template in Artisteer). The term **static website** can be a little bit embarrassing for you, because it's naturally considered with a "page on which nothing moves". You may think that if you add, for example, a slideshow to a static website, it will cease to be static. This is a very natural and logical way of thinking, but in this case, the commonly used terminology is quite different. By saying static website, we don't think about its content, but about the way the page is generated.

What is CMS

In a static HTML website, the content is hardcoded—it is a part of the code of the page. Such a website consists of numerous HTML files and all of them are written separately, one-by-one. They could be prepared with the use of various tools (more or less simplifying the job), but each file contains both the look definitions and the content. All those files are copied to the web server, which make them available for the visitors. This is the most natural and easy-to-understand kind of website.

A dynamic page is definitely more technically advanced. It doesn't exist as a file, but is generated on-the-fly by the web server. After getting the signal that a particular page is to be displayed, a special kind of software gets the proper content (usually from database) and puts it into an available template. After content and template have been successfully combined, the page is ready and is sent to the browser.

Dynamic website is thus, not a collection of static pages (HTML files), but a software installed on the web server for managing content, templates, and merging them into dynamic pages.

Dynamic websites work slower than their static equivalents because each page must be generated before being displayed. They have more server requirements, because the server not only displays, but also generates the pages.

So what are the advantages? Well, this is for sure a much more universal solution, and "once the software, known as a content management system (CMS), is prepared, it can be used many times, for various websites. Let's recall our definition of a template. I have written that a template is a collection of common, fixed elements of a website, like the background, header, and footer.

Those elements are common for the entire website. What differentiates individual pages is the content. With the use of a CMS, the content is separated from the layout and stored in an external store (usually in the database). Right before the page is displayed, CMS gets the appropriate content and puts it into a template.

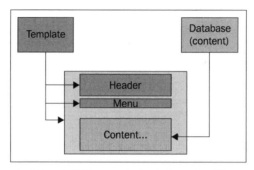

While the page is diplayed, CMS connects fixed elements of the page (template) with proper content from the database

Because the fixed elements are defined only once (they are not duplicated on every page, but exist in only one instance of the template), it means saving of data. But what's even more important is that the separation of look and content allows you to change the template at any time, without any influence to the content. You can change the look of the site at any time and leave the content untouched. If you administer a website or blog over a long period of time, you will surely appreciate such a possibility. The technical separation of appearance and content doesn't mean that you have to enter the content separately, without seeing the template at all (that would be very hard). The more advanced CMS solutions enable you to enter the content online, directly into the browser, with a WYSIWYG editor.

Knowing all the information mentioned earlier, we can form our definition of a CMS.

CMS is a universal software for managing websites. It separates the look of the site from its content by using templates and allows the administrator to enter the content directly into the browser. Usually, CMS systems allow you to manipulate the menu structure, too.

There are various types of CMS available in the market. Some of them are commercial, while others are free, and the possibilities of the most well-known solutions go far beyond our definition. Artisteer supports creating templates for several popular CMSs.

Because content editing has a place directly in the browser, there's no need to upload new pages to the server. It really speeds up managing a website as well as adding new content and pages.

Using CMS system has another, maybe the most important advantage, which is the time needed to add new content to the site.

Imagine that you have a website consisting of 50 pages. (You may think that it's a lot by now, but it's not. After you start to develop your site seriously, you will exceed this number quite easily.) Imagine that it's a static website, consisting of separate HTML documents. The common elements are the header, a vertical menu on the left, and the footer. You want to add just one page and want it to be accessible from the menu. The first step is of course preparing the new page. But after that, you will realize that this was a less time-consuming task (if you use any WYSIWYG editor, you can display the template in it and enter the content very fast). The real problem is with modifying the menu. It's not enough to modify the menu on the page just added, but you will have to modify the menu on all the other pages! (The new page should be accessible from any of the existing pages.) Because the menu is hardcoded on every page (it's just a fragment of their source code), and a static website is just a collection of separate HMTL documents, this means you have to edit and modify all the existing files! In our case, adding one page requires you to modify 50 existing files, and don't forget that you have to also upload all of them onto the server, after your work is finished.

It would be the same situation not only with the menu, but in the case of any fixed element. Do you want to change the phone number in the footer? You have to modify the footer on all pages.

But if you use a CMS, adding a new page is achieved with a few mouse clicks, and the menu adapts automatically to the new site's structure. With the footer, it would be a similar process, and we would need to change it only once. Ease of modification and time savings is what makes CMS the best option for bigger sites.

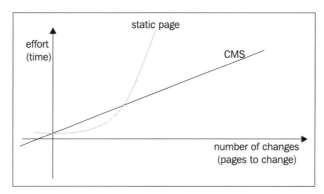

Static website: Adding a single page takes more the time and work, more the pages the site consists of

With a CMS, adding a single page takes less amount of time and work, no matter how big the site is.

Based on the foregoing, flows the following conclusion:

Adding a single page to a static website takes more the time and work, more the pages the website consists of. Adding a single page using a CMS always takes a fixed amount of time and work, no matter how big the entire website is.

But wait! In the previous chapter, we could clearly observe that after adding a page to the project, the menu gets adopted automatically too. Same is the case with the footer or header (fixed elements of layout).

It's true that Artisteer acts similar to a CMS, and this is one of its most important advantages. But note that even when using Artisteer, after changes are done, you will still have to upload all the modified files to the server (and replace the old ones).

Can Artisteer be considered as an alternative for CMS? Well, for small websites, yes. You can use Artisteer features both for designing the template and entering the content, having all together in one tool. But administration of bigger sites will be easier with the use of CMS because you won't have to upload all the modified files onto the server. There are also things that cannot be done in Artisteer alone (for example, sending a message using a **Contact** form). Does this mean that CMS is better than Artisteer? Not in the least, it's just a different kind of tool. CMS is a software for managing websites, while Artisteer is a software for designing templates.

Preparing a template for CMS is more difficult than preparing a template for a static website. Every CMS has its own rules for creating templates, and a template for CMS must contain not only HTML/CSS code, but also some code written in a programming language. Those pieces of additional code are necessary for CMS to know what kind of content should be connected with a particular area in the template.

But don't worry, we have good news, Artisteer can generate templates to various CMSs automatically! That's why the question of what is better: CMS or Artisteer has one proper answer, that is, both. The most comfortable way of designing and managing a bigger website is to:

- Use Artisteer for designing the template (and maybe fill it with initial content)
- Export the template into CMS
- Use CMS for managing the site

Static page template versus CMS template

CMS template creation is a different process from creating templates for static websites, and requires consideration from a different point of view. Let's try to describe in detail the differences between those two cases, and keep in mind some hints that can be useful.

Focus on the design. The content is out of scope.

When designing a static site, you do it usually considering the concrete, or at least planned content. Think about what we did in the previous chapter. We started with the preparation of the scheme that showed the structure of the site. We knew all the subpages it will consist of and what content will be presented on every page. On this basis, we made the decision that the main menu will be a horizontal one, and that we will also have the complementary vertical menu. In the case of the CMS template, the situation looks quite different; often you will not even know what kind of content will be published. You can't assume that the site administrator will use your template according to your assumptions. Nor can you prepare the template based on your own plans about the possible content. Such an approach would limit the site owner. That's why, when creating a template for CMS system, you should focus on the design, not on the content.

To better illustrate what I mean by "approach focused on design, not on the content", let's consider a concrete template element, that is, vertical menu. At the beginning of this chapter, I wrote that particular pages consist of fixed template elements, and the variable factor, content. The content differs from one page to another. This is true. But if we consider the nature of some fixed elements, we realize they are not absolutely fixed. The menu contains links for existing pages. If CMS lets us not only to edit existing pages, but also delete and add new ones, the menu must also be adjusted to the site's changing structure. Every time a new page is added, a new menu item should appear (at the right place!), and when a page is deleted, the corresponding menu item should be deleted with it.

Otherwise, it might happen that the page just added won't have the corresponding item in the menu, so the visitor will not be able to browse to it. Or that menu will still contain the item of a page that has been deleted.

In the case of a static website, you can design the menu as a whole. You know the exact number and titles of the items. You can adjust the size of buttons to item number and make the menu take exactly as much place on the screen as you want. In the case of designing a CMS template, you don't know how many items the menu will contain. You can't predict the size of the menu, because after a new page is added, a new button in the menu will appear making your vertical menu higher. The only solution is to think about the vertical menu as an overall area, filled with items (menu buttons). You can, and you should design the look of the particular menu item, the border of the whole menu, the font of the menu header, but it will still be an overall template and not a concrete menu. You have to accept the fact that you don't have all the information, and you have to do your job despite this. This is what I mean by writing that you should focus on the design, not on the content.

 Template elements lead to completeness of the project.

Because you don't know the content that will be published using your template, you can't limit your job only to designing elements that you know will appear. Your template must be complete and should enable the user to enter every possible kind of content. Your template should provide a uniform look for the entire site. You can't omit some elements, because you don't know if they will be used or not.

For example, while designing the static template in *Chapter 2, The Template Step-by-Step*, we had omitted the third level of headers. We knew the content and that such elements won't be used; so, there wasn't a need to design them. But while designing a CMS template, you can't do that. You should design all possible elements that can occur.

In particular, remember to design:

- Complete typography (headers on all six levels, links in all states, normal text font, quotation, and so on)
- The look of the tables (table header font, table content font, and border)
- Form controls (buttons, radio buttons, and checkboxes)
- Border and margins of images
- Bullets
- Horizontal and vertical menus (you don't know if the user wants to use one of them or both)

Also, you can't omit the special blocks, which are supported by particular CMSs. The most commonly used special blocks are login form and search field. Although the basic approach of all CMS solutions is similar (like online content editing), particular systems differ from each other. Each system has its own specific and typical uses. To design a good template, you have to know the features and properties of the CMS you design for. Artisteer lets you insert the most common blocks with the use of **Widgets** list (it's located on the **Layout** tab on the ribbon). It's not a bad idea to check this list to assure yourself that you didn't forget something important.

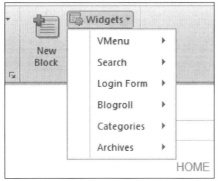

If your target CMS uses one of these blocks,
you should account it in your project

 The knowledge of possibilities and properties of concrete CMS is a basic requirement that allows you to produce a good template for it.

Most modern CMS solutions have a modular design. It means that the core functionality can be expanded by installing extensions. There are thousands of various extensions in the market, dedicated to various popular CMSs. They are provided by third-party companies and offer very diverse functionality. Of course, you can't know which plugins the user will use, and your template doesn't have to support them all. The minimum requirement is to design a template that supports all core functionality of a particular CMS.

In most cases, it's a good idea to choose a three-column layout. To understand why, we will have to go back to the explanation of the way a CMS works. We know that the content is inserted into a page before displayed. We also know that some elements (that is, the menus) have dynamic nature, and their look depends on the site's structure, or other system settings. The next feature is that the site administrator can decide if some of the available elements should be displayed at all. The administrator can, for example, decide that the horizontal menu should be displayed on all the pages, while the vertical menu should be displayed only on some of them (as a supplementary menu), and the search field only on the **Home** page. From one perspective, it gives the huge freedom of managing site, but from another one, it shows how complicated is the problem.

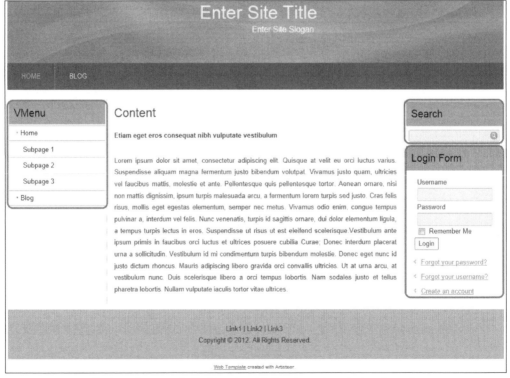

Having columns on both sides gives big freedom when placing elements

Based on the previous information, we can assume that the process of displaying the page through CMS system looks something like this:

1. Get the settings of the page that is going to be displayed.
2. Check which elements should be displayed and which not.
3. Display all the static fixed elements of the template, positioning them into right places.
4. Render dynamic elements of the template, positioning them into right places.
5. Get the proper content, and display it in the content area.

Because dimensions of dynamic elements can change, it is not possible to define their location. You cannot, for example, predict the login field that should be displayed under the vertical menu to be 400 pixels below the top of the page, because we don't know how high the vertical menu will be. The only information we really have is that it should be displayed on the left, under the vertical menu. To solve this problem, CMS templates are based on something we will call **Areas**.

Area is a place in the template, in which you can display a particular element. In Area, you can display various kind of elements, or the Area can be also left empty. A special kind of Area is the Content Area. Content is an element than can occur only once on every page.

Does it mean that other elements can occur several times on the same page, for example two vertical menus, one under another, looking the same? Yes. Even though it would be illogical, it is technically possible.

Areas are always rectangular in shape and they divide a template into rows and columns, so any template can be considered as a grid. The number of cells of this grid (number of areas in template) varies for particular templates.

 A template for a CMS is a combination of available areas and look definitions of elements.

When you write code for your template from the scratch, by hand, you decide about the number and placing of areas. When using Artisteer, you must accept the grid generated by the application.

Artisteer, for CMS systems generates a three-column layout, with Areas in the left and the right column. While designing with Artisteer, you should respect this rule and also base your project on a three-column layout.

Does it mean, that every website based on an Artisteer-generated theme has to have a three-column layout? No. The dimensions of Areas are dynamic—an Area adopts its size to the elements that it contains. The empty Area although exists, but its vertical and horizontal size is zero. From the site administrator's point of view, this is a very good solution, because he has the possibility to display any element in the side column if he wants, but if he doesn't, this column will remain invisible for the visitor.

Designing three-column layouts don't force the user to use all three columns. You give him only the possibility to do this. He still has a free choice to use only one or two of the available columns.

By designing a three-column layout, you give the site administrator the possibility to insert and display any element in side columns. But if he decides not to use these columns at all, they won't even be visible (its width will be zero).

Specific CMS template elements

There are some elements that are specific for CMS templates. Not every CMS system supports all of them. Also, site administrators can decide not to use them, even if they are supported. Nevertheless, if you design a platform that supports these elements, you should include them in your project.

Post header icons

Post header icons are displayed next to the post header. Artisteer supports the **Author**, **Date**, **Edit**, **Email**, **PDF**, and **Print** icons. The last position on the list (**Data**) contains its own subelements.

We will choose the **Print** icon as an example, but the procedure is the same for each icon. To set the **Print** icon, do the following:

1. Select a blog page on the **Pages** panel on the left. If you don't have any, create one. Also, create at least one post to be able to observe the inserted icon.

2. In the **Content** tab on the ribbon, navigate to **Post Header | Icons | Print.** Enable the **Show Print** option. This enables our template to support this icon. After enabling this option, additional options will appear with the collection of available icons. Choose the icon you prefer.

Setting Print icon

Post footer icons

Post footer icons are displayed under the post. Artisteer supports three kinds of these icons, namely **Category**, **Comments**, and **Tags**. The procedure is analogical to inserting post header icons, but instead of the **Post header** button, we use **Post footer**.

We will style **Icons** for **Comments**:

1. Select a blog page on the **Pages** panel on the left. If you don't have any, create one. Also, create at least one post to be able to observe the inserted icon.

2. In the **Content** tab on the ribbon, navigate to **Post Footer | Icons | Comments**. Enable the **Show Comments** option. This makes our template to support this icon. After enabling this option, additional options will appear with the collection of available icons.

3. Choose the icon you prefer.

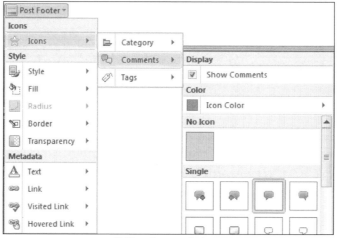

Setting Comments icon

Actually, you don't need a blog page to set up the post icons, but working with a blog page (with at least one post) has the advantage that you immediately see all changes.

Example post in Artisteer, with all icons enabled

Advanced techniques

In this section, we will go through the more advanced functionality in Artisteer that enables you to extend the number of template positions generated by default. But before we start, we will learn how to display the available positions and their names in Joomla!. You will need this information to use additional positions efficiently.

Displaying positions in a Joomla! template

To check the position of a Joomla! Template, do the following:

1. Log in to the Joomla! administrative panel.

2. Navigate to **Extension | Template Manager** from the menu.

3. Click on the **Options** button on the toolbar.

4. Enable the **Preview Module Positions** option.

5. Click on **Save & Close**.

With this function enabled, go to your page, using the address that is in the format `http://address-of-your-site/index.php?tp=1`.

You should see your home page, but its name will be displayed in every template position:

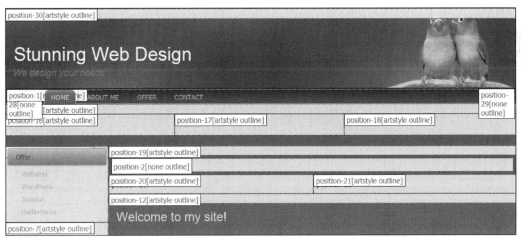

Special address displays positions' names and locations in Joomla!

Additional template position in the header

This functionality applies to Joomla!, WordPress, and Drupal templates.

You can add a new position in the header area. This is handy if you need a special position to show in the header's additional menu, image link (logo), and so on. You can add only one position in the header. In our example, we use .artx project from *Chapter 2, The Template Step-by-Step*:

1. Choose the **Header** tab on the ribbon.

2. Click on the **Controls** button (in the **Insert** group) and select **Position** from the list.

Inserting new area into the header

3. Click anywhere within the header area.

The new position will be inserted in the place you have clicked. You can move it and resize using the mouse, like any other shape.

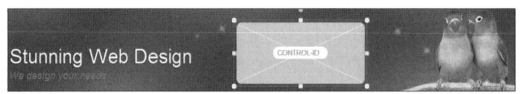

Our header with new template position inserted

You can't insert something into this position using Artisteer, but after exporting template to CMS (that is, Joomla!), this position can be used as any another.

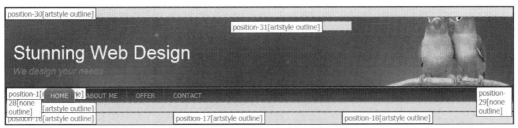

Our new, empty position-31 in Joomla!

Some content inserted into our new position (as Custom HTML module, Joomla!)

Additional template positions in the footer

This functionality applies to Joomla! and WordPress templates.

You can also insert new template positions into the footer. It's very easy. You edit the footer area just like the page's content, inserting new rows and cells, using tools from the **Edit** tab.

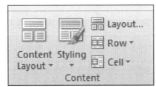

Buttons from Content group on the ribbon's
Edit tab work also for the footer

Footers containing many rows and cells won't be exported as one template position, but Artisteer will create new template positions for each cell.

The following screenshot contains an example grid in the project's footer. All cells will be exported as template positions:

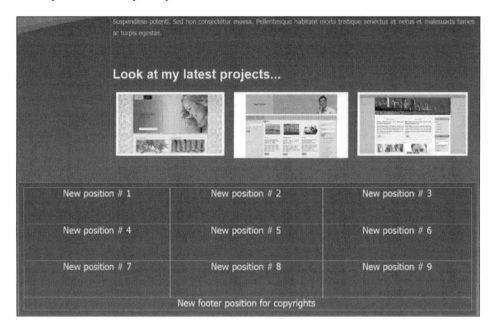

The exported footer's cells that are available Widget Areas in WordPress are as follows:

The exported footer's cells that are available module positions in Joomla! are as follows:

position-32[artstyle outline] n-32	position-33[artstyle outline] on-33	position-34[artstyle outline] n-34
position-35[artstyle outline] n-35	position-36[artstyle outline] on-36	position-37[artstyle outline] n-37
position-38[artstyle outline] n-38	position-39[artstyle outline] on-39	position-40[artstyle outline] n-40
position-41[artstyle outline]	position-41	

This feature, introduced in Artisteer 4.1, shows all the possibilities when you stop to think about the footer as a place not only for inserting copyrights, but when you treat this area as "everything below the main content". There are kinds of websites (especially multimedia portals), in which the layout is a custom grid of different modules/widgets. You can achieve such a template with Artisteer by designing any grid of positions. Remember that the dimensions of template areas adapt to the content they display, and the dimensions of empty areas are zero. According to your needs, you may decide to use one, several, or all areas you have created. You can even decide not to display any article at all, hiding the main Content Area and using only this grid for displaying modules/widgets.

Joomla! templates

Joomla! is a very popular CMS, written in PHP language. To be able to use it, you will need a hosting account that supports PHP and access to one database on MySQL database server. Joomla! is a free, open source software, licensed under the terms of GPL 2, which simply means that you can use it free of charge for commercial purposes too (you can find text of this license at `http://www.gnu.org/licenses/gpl-2.0.html`). You can download the newest version of Joomla! installer from `www.joomla.org`. While I'm writing this book, the newest, long-term, stable version is 2.5.9, and this is the version we are going to work with in this chapter.

Template Areas

Artisteer-generated Joomla! templates contain the following Areas:

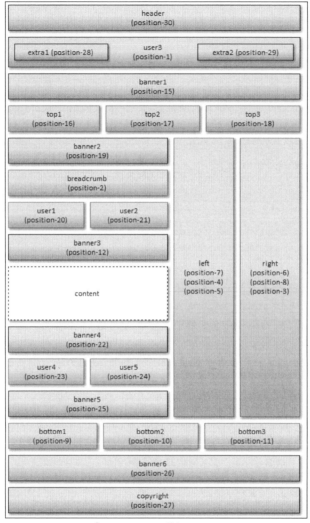

Source: www.artisteer.com

If you look closely at the figure, you will see that every area has two names. The first name is associated with the area's destination, while the second name is given in brackets and is built on the position-number pattern (that is, **position-30**). The first convention was a standard in Joomla! 1.5 (which is still a very popular release), the second was introduced with version 1.6. Because Artisteer exports templates for various versions (1.5 or 2.5-3.0), you can choose the target version of Joomla! and the name convention for template areas while exporting the template.

Exporting a Joomla! template

Exporting of CMS template goes very similar to exporting static page templates that we did in the previous chapter.

The first thing to do is to choose a target platform—in this case Joomla! To do this, click on the arrow beside the **Export** button located in the Quick Access Toolbar of the Ribbon (you can also choose **File | Export | Joomla Template** from the menu).

The **Export** window will appear as follows:

Set the following fields:

- **Template: Joomla Template** (target platform for template)
- **Version: 2.5** (target Joomla! version)
- **Positions: position-1, p...** (Areas' naming convention. We chose the newer one, default for Joomla! 1.6+)
- **FileName:** MyJoomlaTemplate (template filename)
- **Path:** C:\Users\Jakub\Desktop (destination path of a created file. In this case, my desktop)

There are three important options under **Path:** that you can check:

- **ZIP archive**
- **Include ARTX Project**
- **Include Content**

Checking the first one, **ZIP archive**, causes the generated files to be automatically compressed into a ZIP archive. You definitely should check this option, because a ZIP archive is the correct format supported by Joomla! for installing new templates. Such templates can be installed directly from the Joomla! administrative panel.

> You should always check the **ZIP archive** option when exporting for Joomla!.

Checking the option **Include ARTX Project** causes the native Artisteer project file (`.artx`) to be added to exported files. This has no influence on installing or working with the template, and the choice is up to you.

The last option (**Include Content**), introduced in Artisteer 4.0, allows you to export all the content—the pages, text, menu, images, and footer—you have entered in Artisteer along with the template. If your job is to build the entire website and you have entered the final content in Artisteer, checking this option may be a good idea (thanks to this, you won't have to reenter it once again, this time in Joomla!). If your job is just to create the template, you probably won't check this option (although, providing the template with an example content, to show the end user the potential of your template, may be a good idea).

Installing a Joomla! template

Installation of an Artisteer-generated template is done in exactly the same way as installation of any other template. After logging in to administrative panel, do the following:

1. Navigate to **Extensions | Extension Manager** in the menu.
2. In the **Upload Package File** field, click on the **Browse** button.
3. In the open dialog box, point to your template file.
4. Click on **Upload & Install**.

After pointing to your template file, click Upload & Install to install the template

The template will be sent from your local computer to the server (it can take some time, according to the quality of your Internet connection), and will be installed. At the end of this operation, the confirmation text **Installing template was successful** will be shown.

But, when you refresh your site, you will see no changes. Our template is installed, but is not set to be displayed (you can install as many templates as you wish in Joomla!; you may even set up which template should be used to display which page).

Our next step will be to activate our template.

5. To set our template as default:

   ° From the menu, navigate to **Extensions | Template Manager**. You will be redirected to the **Template Manager: Styles** screen.

   ° Find your template on the list and click on the corresponding star on the right (in the **Default** column). The icon (star) will fill itself, which means that from this moment our template is the default one.

6. Refresh the page. You will see that the site is displayed with the use of our template, although some key elements, like menu, aren't displayed. Don't worry, we will fix this problem soon!

Setting up the template

It's time to make our template look like the one we designed in Artisteer.

Title and Slogan

The first elements missing that we are going to display are the Title and Slogan in the header. The text that you have entered for the Title and Slogan in Artisteer are not exported with the template. What is exported is the style (look) of these text, but you have to enter them in Joomla! once again. Let's go back to the Joomla! Administration Panel and perform the following steps:

1. From menu, navigate to **Extensions | Template Manager**. We will go back to the **Template Manager: Styles** screen.

2. Click on your template in the Style column area. You will go into the **Template Manager: Edit Style** screen.

3. On the right-hand side, you will see the **Basic Options** area, with the fields **Headline** and **Slogan**. Enter the appropriate text in them.

4. Click on the **Save** button on the toolbar to save the changes.

After refreshing the page, you will see the Title and Slogan being displayed.

Entering text for Headline and Slogan

Horizontal menu

The creation of a horizontal menu for an Artisteer-generated template looks the same as creation of a horizontal menu for any other template in Joomla! The only thing you must remember is to place it in the position-1 (user3) area.

 If you place horizontal menu in another area, it will work, but it won't look as designed. To make them look as in Artisteer, you have to place it in the position-1 (user3) area.

Vertical menu

The vertical menu is usually placed in the left or right column. The creation of the vertical menu involves some more steps than the horizontal menu, because you have to define a suffix module for it.

To display the vertical menu correctly, including the entire look designed in Artisteer, perform the following steps:

1. Create a new vertical menu module.
2. Place the menu in the target area (usually left or right column).
3. Edit module settings, and in the **Module Manager** screen expand the **Advanced Options** area.
4. In the **Module Class Suffix** field, enter art-vmenu.
5. Save the changes.

To display the vertical menu correctly, you have to set Module Class Suffix as art-vmenu

Footer modification

The last thing to modify is the footer of our site. In Artisteer-generated templates, you can achieve this by modifying **position-27** (copyright) area. All we need to do is create a new module of the Custom HTML kind, and place it in this area. Our module will become the new site footer. Let's perform the following steps:

1. Create a new **Custom HTML** module and give it the **Title**: Footer.
2. Disable displaying module title.
3. Put it in **position-27** (copyrights).
4. Enter the text you want to have in the footer.
5. Save the changes and enable the new module.

Footer module settings

Example text in the footer—of course, you should put your data here

After page refresh, you will see that our site has the new footer, which we have already designed.

Importing content

I'm sure you have marked the **Import Content from Template** button while entering text for the header Headline and Slogan. We are going to use it now and import the content from Artisteer template into a Joomla! site. Perform the following steps:

1. In the Joomla! Administration Panel, navigate to **Extensions | Template Manager**.

2. Go to **Template Manager | Styles** and look for and click on your template, within the **Style** column.

3. In the **Template Manager: Edit Style** screen, click on **Import Content From Template** button.

4. Click on **Import** in the confirmation dialog box.

Click on the Import button to import the content from the template into Joomla!

All the content you have entered in Artisteer will be imported to Joomla!. Horizontal menu, vertical menu, footer, and pages will be automatically created and displayed. Even the Lightbox effect for our images works!

We can observe the way the content was imported:

- A new category called `Articles` was created. All imported articles (text from all pages) have been put into this new category.

- A new module for the horizontal menu has been created, with the name `Content/Horizontal Menu`, and all the items are of Single Article type.

- A new module for the vertical menu has been created, with the name `Content/Vertical Menu`, and all the items are of Single Article type.

- A menu by the name `Content/Special Menu` has been created, but without any associated module. This menu contains two standard items. The first item is of the Category Blog type, associated with articles from the Featured category. The second one is a Single Article item, currently not associated to any article.

- The footer has been imported as a new Custom HTML module, with a name **Footer** that has been placed in **position-27**. Some new empty pages have been added (as articles without any content). Joomla! doesn't allow you to save empty articles. So if you tried to edit and save them unchanged, there will be an error text displayed informing you that you have to enter some content first.

- All the images have been put in `Media`, in the `template-content` folder.

- A block containing our contact information has been inserted as a new module of the Custom HTML type.

Also note that both aliases of menu items and articles show neither titles nor file names for pages that we entered in Artisteer. Menu aliases are created with the use of *ct-menu-item-number* pattern.

 For SEO purposes, you should modify aliases in imported articles and menu items.

WordPress templates

WordPress is another very popular CMS, written in PHP language. To use it, you will need a hosting account with support for PHP and access to one MySQL database. You can also sign up for your free instance of the system at the `wordpress.com` domain. The software is released under the GPL license and you can download it for free from the official project page `wordpress.org`. WordPress is the successor of b2/cafelog blogging system, and initially was also a blogging platform. With time and new releases, the system has matured and by now it can be considered as a full CMS system.

What differentiates WordPress from other solutions is its ease of use and administration, making WordPress one of the best choices for beginners. Not only is WordPress a very user-friendly solution, but also the system's core functionality can be extended with various plugins (there are thousands of them on the market, both free and commercial), making this CMS an extendable solution, appropriate for many projects. At the time of writing this book, the latest WordPress version available is 3.5.1.

Widget areas

Like other CMS systems, WordPress templates have special areas to place special elements (called **widgets**). Artisteer exports WordPress themes with the following widget areas:

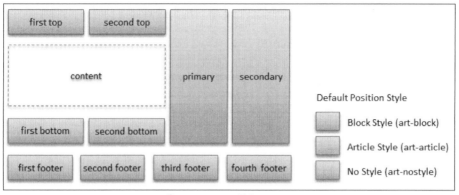

Source: www.artisteer.com

Exporting a WordPress template

When exporting a template for WordPress, you have to choose WordPress as the target platform. Make sure that in the **Export** window, **WordPress Theme** is chosen in the **Template** field.

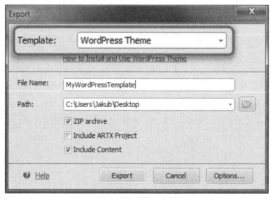

Exporting WordPress theme

The rest of the settings are analogical, such as export for Joomla!. Make sure that the **ZIP archive** option is checked. This will allow you to install the template directly from the WordPress Administration Panel.

You can also click on the **Options** button and set WordPress-specific settings. There are not plenty of them. You can define the text for Home Page in menu item, and whether this item should be displayed or not.

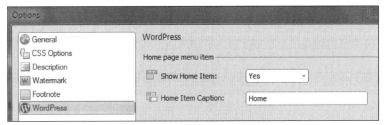

WordPress related export options

After you export a WordPress template, it's then time to install it into the CMS:

1. Log into Administration Panel.
2. From the menu, navigate to **Appearance | Themes**.
3. Click on the **Install Themes** tab (on top of the screen).
4. Click on the **Upload** link.
5. Click on the **Browse** button, point to the exported theme file, and click on **Install Now**.

Installing new template in WordPress

After a while, the template is installed, but if we want it to be displayed, we have to activate it.

6. Click on the **Activate** link. If you refresh the site, you will see that it's displayed with our template.

Setting up the template

Now, when our template is installed and activated, it's time to set it up.

Title and slogan

The first thing that we are going to do is to set up the correct title and slogan for our page. To do this, perform the following steps (we assume you're logged into WordPress control panel):

1. Navigate to **Appearance | Themes** from the menu.
2. Find your template and click on the **Customize** link.
3. Click on the **Site Title & Tagline** option.
4. Enter the correct title in the **Site Title** field and slogan in the **Tagline** field.

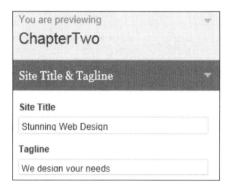

5. Click on the **Save & Publish** button.

Customizing the footer

If your template is imported and activated, you can customize the footer of the site. To do this, log in to Administration Panel and from the main menu on the left, navigate to **Appearance | Theme options**. Then in the main screen area, scroll down and find the **Footer** section. Click on **Override default theme footer content** and enable the field below. Now you can enter any content for the footer you want to have. Because it's not a WYSIWYG editor, you need to write HTML tags by hand.

Menus

Creation of horizontal and vertical menus for Artisteer-generated template looks the same as the menus for any other template in WordPress.

Importing content

If you checked the **Include Content** option by exporting the template from Artisteer after you have installed and activated the template, you will be asked if you want to import the content from the template:

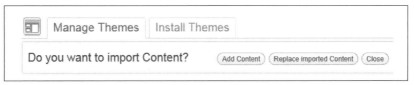

Importing content from Artisteer-generated template to WordPress

According to what you want to do, you can decide to add the imported content to the content that already exists in WordPress, to replace existing content, or just click on the **Close** button and refuse importing content. We click on **Replace imported Content**.

After a while, our content will be imported and put into the CMS. You can refresh the page and see that the content is available and displayed.

We can see that the content has been imported and is displayed in the following manner:

- All normal pages from Artisteer project have been imported as Pages. All pages have correctly set up Parent property. Site's structure is preserved.
- All Blog posts from Artisteer have been imported as Posts. All posts belong to the Uncategorized category.

Two menus has been created, namely, Sample HMenu (horizontal menu) and Sample VMenu (vertical menu). Pages and Posts have been associated with the menus of other CMS systems.

We have described installing and importing content for Joomla! and WordPress, because they are both very popular solutions. However, Artisteer supports more CMS systems, and with the SDK being introduced in Artisteer 4, there is a possibility to extend the number of supported systems. We can expect that the number of supported CMSs will increase.

The overall way of installing Artisteer and non-Artisteer templates in a particular CMS is the same; so, it's rather a question of operating with a certain CMS solution than with Artisteer itself.

The most important thing you should know while designing for a particular CMS is the layout of the template areas that Artisteer generates for various platforms.

Drupal

Artisteer-generated templates contain the following areas in Drupal themes:

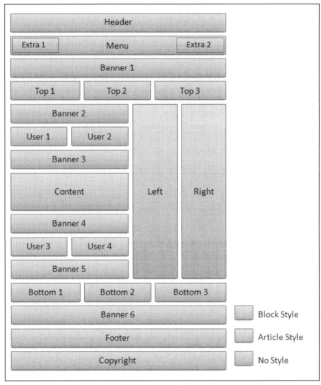

Source: www.artisteer.com

DotNetNuke

Artisteer-generated templates contain the following areas in DotNetNuke themes:

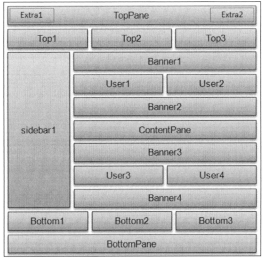

Source: www.artisteer.com

Content editing – Artisteer or CMS

We have automatically imported all the content from our Artisteer project into Joomla! and WordPress. All that we have prepared in Artisteer — that is, pages (with text and pictures), menus, menu items, and the footer — exists now and works correctly in our CMS site. While the entire process is easy and very fast, you may wonder what the best way of working is: should you prepare all the content in Artisteer and then import it into CMS, or should you install the empty template and enter the content directly in CMS?

The answer to this question is not so obvious. Both methods work and it's up to you to choose any one. But you should consider the advantages and disadvantages of each method. The following are the advantages and disadvantages of preparing content directly in Artisteer:

Advantages of preparing content in Artisteer	Disadvantages of preparing content in Artisteer
Can be done very fast, without the need of switching to CMS or even installing it. You can do it before having a hosting account.	The content is imported according to the rules imposed by Artisteer. You have no choice but to accept them. For example, in WordPress, all the posts will be put into one category called Uncategorized.
As long as content remains within the Artisteer project, it remains platform-independent (omitting, of course, platform-specific features). You can prepare the entire website before making the decision of using a particular CMS.	You can't set up some important properties, for example, aliases for articles and menu items in Joomla!. They are set automatically. This has a direct influence to SEO addresses. If you want to fix them, you have to correct it by hand, in the CMS. This takes time.
If you prepare a website for someone else, you can prepare the whole site with content, without even touching his system. You can just export the entire site as one installable ZIP package.	You cannot use functionality provided by any third-party extension that you have installed in your CMS, or use images that you have already been uploaded. You are outside the destination system.
You can prepare sample content for your template.	

And the following are the advantages and disadvantages of preparing content directly in CMS:

Advantages of preparing content directly in CMS	Disadvantages of preparing content directly in CMS
You can use all the power of your CMS, including all installed extensions and uploaded images.	Web applications are less responsive than desktop applications. You will probably need a little less time to write a simple article using Artisteer than with CMS.
You have complete control over the content and CMS features. You can set proper aliases for articles and menu items, assign various articles with various categories, set category names, location for uploaded images, and so on.	
Content can be inserted by a team of people simultaneously.	

The conclusion that we can draw from the above analysis is that if you make a simple website, or have to do something very fast, you can prepare the content in Artisteer and then import it into CMS system. In case you build a rather complicated website and you have already decided about which CMS you want to use, entering the content directly in the CMS is a better option. You will have full control over your work.

Summary

In this chapter, you have learned how to design templates for CMS platforms. We have discussed the overall differences between CMS-powered and static HTML website, and got to know some new features of Artisteer. We have successfully exported and installed templates in Joomla! and WordPress—two of the most popular CMS solutions.

But our adventure with Artisteer does not finish yet. With little changes in the generated code, you can achieve "apparently-impossible-to-do-in-Artisteer" things.

4
Tips and Tricks

We have gone through most of the Artisteer features and you can by now design and use your own templates. The last thing to cover is some tips and tricks—techniques that will allow us to achieve effects, not available in Artisteer directly. They would require a little modification of the exported code, but don't worry, the changes won't be difficult, and I will always describe the changes. The examples here are the common questions that I have been asked by many Artisteer users. I'm sure you will have your own questions too. A good source of tips and tricks is the subscription of the Extensoft newsletter, in which some nice tips are published. Also a good source of knowledge is Artisteer's official website `www.artisteer.com` and Szablonik (`www.szablonik.net`)—another website devoted to Artisteer. You may also look at my blog: `http://artisteer.fajnyblog.eu`, where I publish tips from time-to-time.

Image links in a slideshow

This tip applies to HTML templates. An example project would be the `slidesAsLinks.artx` file.

In this tip, I will show you how to modify the slideshow to make each slide (or some of them, it's up to you) linked to other websites.

When you create a slideshow, you can define particular images, but you can't set any of the slides as links. The first idea is of course to click anywhere in the article and then navigate to **Edit | HTML** in the menu to show the source of the article containing the slideshow and do the proper modification without going out of the program. Let's do it.

1. In place of the slideshow, you will find something like the following:

```
<div class="image-caption-wrapper" style="width: 55%;
float: left">
[collage_79]
</div>
```

Downloading the example code

You can download the example code files for all Packt books you have purchased from your account at http://www.packtpub.com. If you purchased this book elsewhere, you can visit http://www.packtpub.com/support and register to have the files e-mailed directly to you.

2. Oops! It looks like Artisteer presents the slideshow not as source code, but as a special tag. The whole slideshow is presented as [collage_79] (the number may differ, but the overall pattern is always the same).

3. Well, we have no other choice but to export the template, and then edit the source. Export the template as a folder and open the index.html file in the text editor. Look for the part of code responsible for displaying the slideshow. You will find something similar to the following:

```
<div class="art-slider art-slidecontainer79">
  <div class="art-slider-inner">
    <div class="art-slide-item art-slide790"></div>
    <div class="art-slide-item art-slide791"></div>
    <div class="art-slide-item art-slide792"></div>
    <div class="art-slide-item art-slide793"></div>
  </div>
</div>
```

4. Let's add some comments to the code to make it more clear:

```
<!-- The external container, containing the slideshow -->
<div class="art-slider art-slidecontainer79">
  <!-- slideshow container -->
  <div class="art-slider-inner">
    <!-- first slide -->
    <div class="art-slide-item art-slide790"></div>
    <!-- second slide -->
    <div class="art-slide-item art-slide791"></div>
    <!-- third slide -->
    <div class="art-slide-item art-slide792"></div>
    <!-- forth slide -->
    <div class="art-slide-item art-slide793"></div>
  </div>
</div>
```

The slideshow is displayed as two containers, and the inner one contains its own inner containers—in particular, slides. Each slide is represented as a `<div>` element (before the jQuery script in the `<header>` section does its job).

5. To make each slide a link, we are going to add some basic JavaScript to each slide; specifically, we are going to handle `onClick` events (in other words, we will define what should happen when a visitor clicks on this `<div>` element representing a particular slide). Because this is only a single-line script, there's no need to separate it as a `<script>` element in the code.

We are going to add something according to the following pattern:

```
onclick=location.href('address_to_be_redirected_to')
```

For example:

```
onclick=location.href('www.google.com')
```

This `onclick` event will redirect the visitor to `www.google.com`.

6. Let's modify our code and add the links:

```
<div class="art-slider art-slidecontainer79">
  <!-- The external container, containing the slideshow -->
<div class="art-slider art-slidecontainer79">
  <!-- Slideshow container -->
  <div class="art-slider-inner">
    <!-- First slide. Link to: www.artisteeer.com -->
    <div class="art-slide-item art-
slide790"onclick="location.href='http://www.artister.com'"
></div>
    <!-- Second slide. Link to: www.google.com -->
    <div class="art-slide-item art-slide791"
onclick="location.href='http://www.google.com'"></div>
    <!-- Third slide. Link to: www.example.com -->
    <div class="art-slide-item art-slide792"
onclick="location.href='http://www.example.com'"></div>
    <!-- Forth slide. Link to www.packtpub.com -->
    <div class="art-slide-item art-slide793"
onclick="location.href='http://www.packtpub.com'"></div>
  </div>
</div>
```

7. Save the file and view it in a browser. The slides now act as links. The solution works, but it would be useful to have the mouse pointer indicate that there is a link. We will achieve this with a little bit of CSS, setting the appearance of the mouse cursor. We need to add the following text to each slide definition:

```
style="cursor: pointer;"
```

8. After modifications, we will have the following code:

```
<!-- The external container, containing the slideshow -->
<div class="art-slider art-slidecontainer79">
  <!-- Slideshow container -->
  <div class="art-slider-inner">
    <!-- First slide. Link to: www.artisteer.com -->
    <div class="art-slide-item art-slide790"
onclick="location.href='http://www.artisteer.com'"
style="cursor: pointer;"></div>
    <!-- Second slide. Link to: www.google.com -->
    <div class="art-slide-item art-slide791"
onclick="location.href='http://www.google.com'"
style="cursor: pointer;"></div>
    <!-- Third slide. Link to: www.example.com -->
    <div class="art-slide-item art-slide792"
onclick="location.href='http://www.example.com'"
style="cursor: pointer;"></div>
    <!-- Forth slide. Link to www.packtpub.com -->
    <div class="art-slide-item art-slide793"
onclick="location.href='http://www.packtpub.com'"
style="cursor: pointer;"></div>
  </div>
</div>
```

9. It's much better! The last thing we should do is add a hint to inform the visitor about which page he/she will be redirected to. To do this, we need to add a title parameter to each `<div>` representing a slide as follows:

```
title="description of the link"
```

10. Our final code looks as follows:

```
<!-- The external container, containing the slideshow -->
<div class="art-slider art-slidecontainer79">
  <!-- Slideshow container -->
  <div class="art-slider-inner">
    <!-- First slide. Link to: www.artisteer.com -->
    <div class="art-slide-item art-slide790"
onclick="location.href='http://www.artisteer.com'"
style="cursor: pointer;" title="Artisteer official
page"></div>
    <!-- Second slide. Link to: www.google.com-->
    <div class="art-slide-item art-slide791"
```

```
onclick="location.href='http://www.google.com'"
style="cursor: pointer;" title="Search engine"></div>
    <!-- Third slide. Link to: www.example.com -->
    <div class="art-slide-item art-slide792"
onclick="location.href='http://www.example.com'"
style="cursor: pointer;" title="Example domain"></div>
    <!-- Forth slide. Link to www.packtpub.com -->
    <div class="art-slide-item art-slide793"
onclick="location.href='http://www.packtpub.com'"
style="cursor: pointer;" title="Visit Packt
Publishing"></div>
  </div>
</div>
```

11. That's all. After the modifications, each link in our slideshow is a link to another webpage. The mouse cursor is the shape of a hand, which is typical for hyperlinks. Besides, there's a short description about where you will be redirected to.

Our slide with link description

Removing the vertical menu from some pages

This tip applies to HTML templates. An example project would be the `chapterTwo.artx` project file.

In *Chapter2, The Template Step-by-Step*, we prepared a template with horizontal and vertical menus. The horizontal menu was the main menu of our site, showing the items related with directly linked pages, and the vertical menu was a complementary one, showing details of our offer. We came to the conclusion that the best way of organizing menus would be to show the vertical menu only on pages that are sub-pages of the **Offer** page. This would be better and more logical than to display details of our offer on every page.

Unfortunately, Artisteer doesn't allow us do define on which pages a menu should be displayed, and both the menus are displayed on every page. The way to work around this limitation is to create the template with both the menus (as we did) and then remove the vertical menu from the pages in which we don't want it to be displayed. This way we will make the vertical menu act as a submenu of the horizontal menu Let's begin:

1. Let's export the project from *Chapter 2, The Template Step-by-Step* once again and then open the index.html file (the home page of our site).

2. Now look at the files that Artisteer has created. You will see four .html files that are pages on the top level of the site structure, namely, home, about me, offer, and contact.

3. The subpages of the **Offer** page are located in a separate folder called Offer. The structure of folders and files reflects the site's logical structure. That makes our task simpler. All the .html files located in the Offer folder should display the vertical menu, while we should delete it from .html files located in the main project folder.

4. Let's open the index.html file and search for the vertical menu in the code. You will find something like the following:

```
<div class="art-vmenublockcontent">
<ul class="art-vmenu">
<li>
<a href="offer.html">Offer</a>
<ul>
    <li>
    <a href="offer/websites.html">Websites</a>
    </li>
    <li>
    <a href="offer/wordpress.html">WordPress</a>
    </li>
    <li>
    <a href="offer/joomla.html">Joomla!</a>
    </li>
    <li>
    <a href="offer/dotnetnuke.html">DotNetNuke</a>
    </li>
    </ul>
  </li>
</ul>
</div>
```

We see that the main container of the entire vertical menu is a `<div>` element, with the `art-vmenublockcontent` class. This is the key information for our task. Then the menu items are a list. The next level of menu items is represented as the next level of this list.

5. To remove the vertical menu from the page, just remove the main menu container with all of its content (the previous code). Now, save the file and refresh the page in the browser. We see that the vertical menu has disappeared from the **HOME** page.

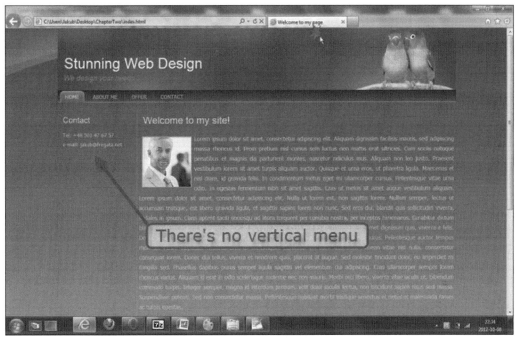

We have removed the vertical menu from the HOME page

6. Great! Now, repeat the whole operation for the rest of our top-level sites, that is, the `about me.html`, `offer.html`, and `contact.html` files.

   As a result, we don't have the vertical menu on these pages any more.

7. Because we haven't touched the pages from the `Offer` folder, the subpages or the **Offer** page (**Websites**, **WordPress**, **Joomla!**, and **DotNetNuke**) display the vertical menu.

8. Our job is already done, but if you take a closer look at the vertical menu, you will see that it displays two levels of items as shown in the following screenshot:

Our vertical menu displays two levels of items

9. The first level contains only one item, **Offer**. We had to leave this item, because while designing in Artisteer, a menu can't contain only its subitems, without displaying their parent item. But it's obvious that **Offer** is not necessary in this case, so let's look into the code and try to fix it. As we saw in the previous code, in step 4, menu items form the list. Each next level of item is represented as a new, nested list:

```
<!--List representing our menu -->
<ul class="art-vmenu">
<li>
  <!-- First level item - Offer -->
<a href="offer.html">Offer</a>
  <!-- Nested list - next level of items -->
<ul>
<!--- First subitem -->
    <li>
    <a href="offer/websites.html">Websites</a>
    </li>
<!-- Second subitem -->
    <li>
    <a href="offer/wordpress.html">WordPress</a>
    </li>
<!-- Next subitems… -->
    <li>
    <a href="offer/joomla.html">Joomla!</a>
    </li>
    <li>
    <a href="offer/dotnetnuke.html">DotNetNuke</a>
    </li>
    </ul>
  </li>
</ul>
```

10. Let's open the `offer.html` file and change this into a one-level list containing only our subpages. We don't need the first item, **Offer**, so we can delete it. We now have the code as follows:

```html
<!--List representing our menu -->
<ul class="art-vmenu">
  <!-- Nested list - next level of items -->
<ul>
<!-- First subitem -->
    <li>
    <a href="offer/websites.html">Websites</a>
    </li>
<!-- Second subitem -->
    <li>
    <a href="offer/wordpress.html">WordPress</a>
    </li>
<!-- Next subitems… -->
    <li>
    <a href="offer/joomla.html">Joomla!</a>
    </li>
    <li>
    <a href="offer/dotnetnuke.html">DotNetNuke</a>
    </li>
  </ul>
</ul>
```

11. Because we don't have any parent item in our menu anymore, there's no sense to have two nested lists in our code (the `<ul>` tags). Let's delete the internal list. We now get the following code:

```html
<ul class="art-vmenu">
  <li>
  <a href="offer/websites.html">Websites</a>
  </li>
  <li>
  <a href="offer/websites.html">Websites</a>
  </li>
  <li>
  <a href="offer/wordpress.html">WordPress</a>
  </li>
  <li>
  <a href="offer/joomla.html">Joomla!</a>
  </li>
  <li>
  <a href="offer/dotnetnuke.html">DotNetNuke</a>
  </li>
</ul>
```

12. Save the file and refresh the site. Your vertical menu should now be displayed as shown in the following screenshot:

Our vertical menu, displaying only subpages as top level items

Styling a particular module

This tip applies to Joomla! templates. An example would be the `specialModule.artx` file.

This tip is based on standard techniques used in Joomla!, but in the case of Artisteer, it requires some more explanation.

It's quite a common situation that you want to have one of your modules looking different from the others. For example, you may want the login module or some other module to be distinguished from others. In the case of custom HTML modules, you can of course modify HTML directly in the module, but this tip allows you to do it without touching HTML and is based only on CSS modification.

> This technique works for modules taking their CSS from the template stylesheet. It won't work with custom extensions that are rendered separately with their own styles. In such cases, you will have to take a look into the source of a particular extension and modify the code accordingly.

In our example, we will distinguish the login module to make it more eye-catching for visitors.

While designing in Artisteer, you can't make a particular module different from others, as changes spread into the others blocks. That's the reason we need a solution.

We are working on the `specialModule.artx` project with content. Open it and export it to Joomla!. Your site should look like the following screenshot:

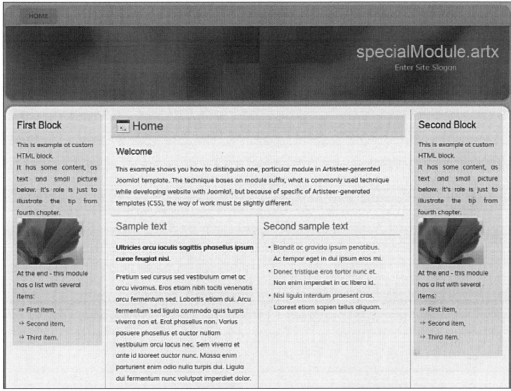

Sample site with two identical modules on the left-hand and right-hand columns

The site contains only one page, has a three-column layout, and two identical modules on the left-hand and right-hand columns. They were imported as two separate custom HTML modules, but both were created in Artisteer. Our task is to distinguish the second module, without modifying its HTML, as follows:

1. In Joomla!'s administrative panel, navigate to **Extensions | Module Manager**. You will go to the **Modules** screen in **Module Manager**, which will present all installed modules. Find and click on the **Second Block** module to go to its settings.

2. In **Module Manager: Module Custom HTML** (**Second Block** module settings), expand the **Advanced Options** area and find the **Module Class Suffix** field. In this field, we are going to type a suitable suffix.

3. Type `_SpecialModule` into the **Module Class Suffix** field as shown in the following screenshot:

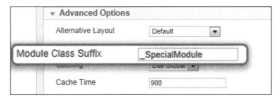

Type _SpecialModule as Module Class Sufix

4. On the basis of the **Module Class Suffix** name you type in this field, Joomla! will search for a new class definition defined in template CSS style. It's done according to the pattern *art-block + space + clearfix + what-you-type-in-the-field*.

    In our case this means *art-block + _SpecialModule = art-block clearfix_ SpecialModule*

    Joomla!, while rendering the page, will look for art-block clearfix_SpecialModule definition in the CSS stylesheet. This means that our block will use styles from two classes: art-block and clearfix_SpecialModule.

    The art-block class is defined originally by Artisteer. Look in the source for this class and analyze it. This class defines the block's background, border, and rounded corners. The fact that our block will get styles from two classes is quite handy — we don't need to define everything from scratch, but only add supplementary definitions. What's more, because our class is defined second, our definitions will cover the original one coming from Artisteer. We can just remove our class any time to revert back to the original look of the template.

5. We need to add our class in the CSS template file. This file is called `template.css` and is located in the CSS folder in the `template` folder. Open this file in the editor and at the end write:

```
/*** My Classes ***/
.custom_SpecialModule
{
border: 1pt solid red;
  background-color: #FFFF99;
}
```

We have overwritten the width and color of the border, and have also set the
background color as a delicate shade of yellow. Save the file and refresh
the page. You should see something like the following screenshot:

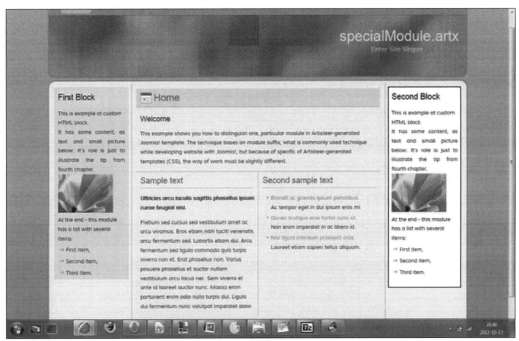

Our block on the right looks quite different from its twin brother on the left

6. So far, so good. Let's perform the next step and change the font of the text.
   Add another line of code to our class and make it look like the following:

```
.clearfix_SpecialModule
{
  border: 1pt solid red;
  background-color: #FFFF99;
  color: blue;
}
```

7. Save the changes, refresh the page, and… nothing happened! Something is
   wrong. Revert the changes (delete the last definition from our class) and then
   let's look at the source code of the page. The piece of code that displays our
   block looks like the following:

```
<div class="art-block clearfix_SpecialModule">
  <div class="art-blockheader">
    <h3 class="t">Second Block</h3>
  </div>
  <div class="art-blockcontent">
    <div class="custom_SpecialModule"  >
```

```
    <!—
content of our block:
<p> elements, image and list
 -->
    </div>
  </div>
</div>
```

So now we need to keep in mind the following rules:

- The DIV element that contains the whole block belongs to the following two classes:
  - art-block
  - clearfix_SpecialModule (according to our suffix)

- The header is inside a DIV element. This element belongs to the art-blockheader class. The header itself is an h3 element and belongs to the t class.

- The content of our block is inside a DIV element. This element belongs to the custom_SpecialModule (according to our suffix) class and is located inside another DIV element, which belongs to the art-blockcontent class.

The structure of our block displays the following scheme:

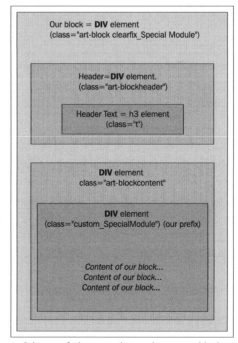

Scheme of elements that make up our block

8. Knowing this, we can write some additional definitions and make our block look a little more different. We will set up the header's color as green, display content text in italics style, change its font style, and add a border to the picture:

```
/*** My Classes ***/
.clearfix_SpecialModule
{
  border: 1pt solid red;
  background-color: #FFFF99;
}

.clearfix_SpecialModule .art-blockheader h3
{
  color: green;
}

.custom_SpecialModule p
{
  font-family: "Tahoma";
  font-style: italic;
}

.clearfix_SpecialModule .custom_SpecialModule img
{
  border: 1px solid #000000;
}
```

OK, we have achieved our goal and made our block look different. But the best advantage of this technique is that after the styles are defined, you can use them for any module, without additional work. To illustrate this, we will remove the styles from our **Second Block** and apply them to the login box:

1. Edit the **Second Block** module in the administration panel and clear the **Module Class Suffix** field. **Second Block** will look again exactly like **First Block**.

2. Create the **Login** module and place it under **Second Block** in the right–hand column. Display the module (**position-7**).

3. Edit preferences of your **Login** module and type _SpecialModule (that's our suffix) in the **Module Class Suffix** field.

4. Save the changes and refresh the site. You will notice that the **Login** module has adopted the styles that we defined previously.

Of course this module contains some unique elements that were not defined, but the overall effect works.

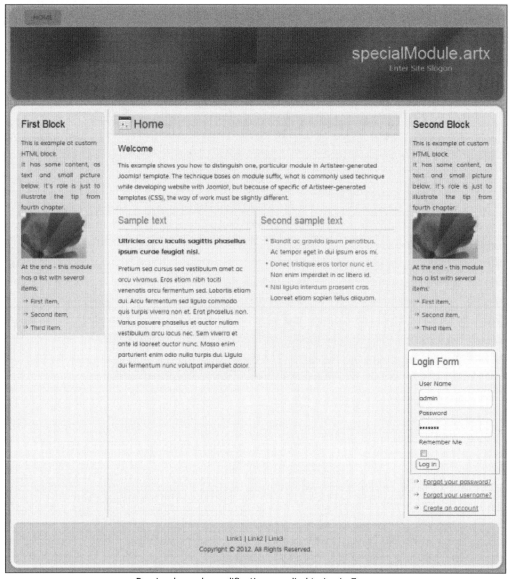

Previously made modifications applied to Login Form

Styling from scratch

In the earlier example, we had styled our **Second Block** mixing our class with the standard `art-block` Artisteer class. But sometimes, you will be more interested in removing all the template styles and styling a particular module from scratch. For such purposes, Artisteer provides a special class called `art-nostyle`. The name of this class should be the first part of your suffix.

> In fact, when you use the `art-nostyle` class to compose your suffix, the module will also get the definitions from two classes, namely, `art-nostyle` and your own (which name comes from the suffix). But the use of the `art-nostyle` class causes the module to be displayed omitting template styles, so in reality the effect is as if the module wasn't styled at all.

In this example, we will work with the same **Second Block** in our project. The steps are as follows:

1. If you have modified the template CSS file according to our previous example, delete the template and install it once again. This will prevent you from having an untidy `template.css` file. Assuming that both **First Block** and **Second Block** look the same, edit the **Second Block** module properties and in the **Module Class Suffix** field type `art-nostyle MySpecialModule`.

2. Save the changes and refresh the site. You will see that our **Second Block** again looks different from the **First Block**, but this time it looks like it wasn't styled at all:

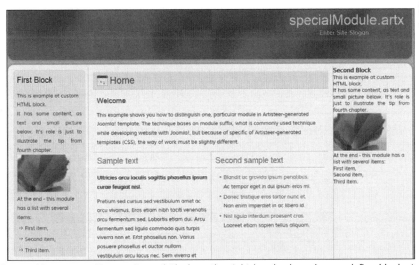

After enabling new suffix, our Second Block on the right-hand column has no defined look at all

This time we didn't start the name of our class in the suffix with the _ character. We didn't do it because when we compose our suffix with one of the predefined Artisteer classes (in this case, `art-nostyle`), the word `clearfix` won't be added to our class name.

3. Using the suffix in this form will cause Joomla!, while rendering our **Second Block**, to seek for both `art-nostyle` and `MySpecialBlock` classes. The first one is a standard Artisteer class. We need to add the second definition to the `template.css` file. But before we do that, let's take a look at the source of the generated page:

```
<!-- begin nostyle -->
<div class="art-nostyle MySpecialModule">
  <h3>Second Block</h3>
  <!-- begin nostyle content -->
    <div class="customart-nostyle MySpecialModule">
      <!--
content of our block:
<p> elements, image and list
      -->
    </div>
  <!-- end nostyle content -->
</div>
<!-- end nostyle -->
```

This time our task is easier because Artisteer inserts comments informing us about the beginning and the end of the unstyled fragment of the page. The whole block resides in a DIV element, which belongs to two classes, namely, `art-nostyle` and `MySpecialModule` (`class="customart-nostyle MySpecialModule"`), according to what we have typed as a suffix in Joomla!. The header of the block is just an h3 element, without any class. The content of our block is in another DIV element, which also belongs to the classes `customart-nostyle` and `MySpecialModule` (`class="customart-nostyle MySpecialModule"`). We would like to compose styles that will make our **Second Block** look similar to our previous example.

4. So, let's open the `template.css` file and add a definition to our classes. Because we have decided not to expand the existing style for block elements (the `art-block` class) but to design everything on our own, we must define more properties than the previous time:

```
/*** My Classes ***/
/* Main container of our block */
.MySpecialModule
```

```
{
  /* rounded corners of main container */
  -webkit-border-radius: 6px 6px 0 0;
  -moz-border-radius: 6px 6px 0 0;
  border-radius: 6px 6px 0 0;
  /* margins, border and background color */
  margin: 7px;
  border: 1pt solid red;
  background-color: #FFFF99;
}

/* Block header */
.MySpecialModule h3
{
  padding: 12px 3px;
  color: green;
  font-size: 20px;
  font-family: Moul, Arial, 'Arial Unicode MS', Helvetica, Sans-
Serif;
  font-weight: normal;
  margin: 0 5px;
}

/* Paragraph in block content */
.MySpecialModule p
{
  font-family: "Tahoma";
  font-size: 10pt;
  font-style: italic;
  line-height: 180%;
}

/* Image border */
.MySpecialModule img
{
  border: 1px solid #000000;
}

/* List inside block content */
.MySpecialModule ul
{
  margin-left: 10px;
}
```

```
.MySpecialModule ul li
{
  list-style-image: url('./images/blockbullets.png');
  margin: 10px 15px;
}
```

5. Save the changes, refresh the site, and the following screenshot will appear:

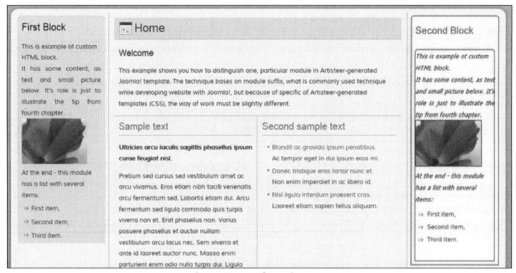

Current state of our changes

6. Everything seems to be quite OK, but we don't want to have the border around the internal DIV element. This border is defined in our .MySpecialModule class and we have to exclude it for our DIV element that contains the content of the block (look of the scheme again). Edit the template.css file once again and append the following code at the end:

```
.customart-nostyle.MySpecialModule
{
  margin-top: 0;
  border: none;
}
```

7. Save the changes and refresh the site. That's it! We have styled our **Second Block** from scratch by combining our module suffix with the built-in Artisteer art-nostyle class.

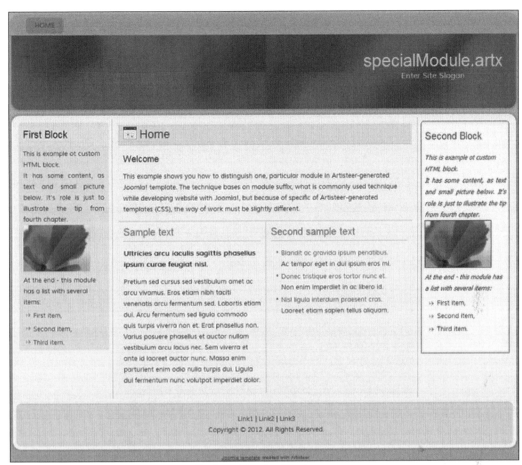

Our template after the changes

Combinations with other Artisteer-generated classes

In the first example, we combined our class with Artisteer-generated class `art-block`. In the second example, we styled our module from scratch, combining our class with the `art-nostyle` Artisteer class. According to your needs, it may be useful to combine the module suffix with other standard Artisteer-generated classes (that is, `art-article`, used for posts). It's a good idea and a good exercise to analyze the `template.css` file of the exported template. It's also a good exercise to analyze the main Joomla! template file entirely (the `index.php` file in your `template` directory) and the source generated by Joomla!. A good understanding of how Artisteer-generated templates are built and how they work is useful when it comes to custom modifications of the templates.

Adding additional CSS to the project

This tip applies to all kinds of templates. In this example, we will work with the HTML template.

If you need to add some of your own CSS to the original template's stylesheet, you can do it directly from Artisteer. This feature may also be useful if you want to modify original Artisteer classes. Here are the steps for this tip:

1. In this example, we work with the `AddCssToProject.artx` project file. Open it. This is the site that we saw in *Chapter 2, The Template Step-by-Step*, but I have added a simple contact form in the **Contact** page.

   In this example, we will add some CSS definitions to achieve three goals:

   ° We want to change the default Artisteer prefix for CSS classes.

   ° We want to distinguish images when moving the mouse cursor over them (roll-over effect). This effect should apply only to images with the Lightbox effect.

   ° We want to distinguish active controls in the **Contact** form.

2. To add CSS to the generated code, click on the **Export** button and in the **Export** window, click on the **Options** button. In the **Options** window that will appear, click on the **CSS Options** pane on the left. The right-hand side of the window will show you the available options. You will see that there are two fields, namely, **CSS Prefix:** and **Additional CSS Styles:**.

   The **CSS Prefix:** field contains the prefix that will be used to name CSS classes generated in the exported template. The default value is `art-`.

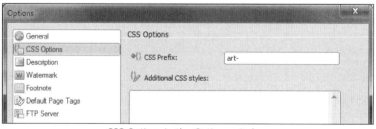

CSS Options in the Options window

3. Recall the standard classes we worked with in the *Styling from scratch* tip. We worked with the `art-block`, `art-nostyle`, and `art-article` classes. The first part of its name is the prefix you type in this field. Let's assume that I would write `jakub-` here (from my name). In such a case, instead of the `art-block`, `art-nostyle`, or `art-article` class, Artisteer would generate the class names, namely, `jakub-block`, `jakub-nostyle`, or `jakub-article`, respectively. Changing the default CSS class prefix doesn't change anything in the code, but class names. So why would you do that? There are two reasons:

   ○ Sometimes you may want to hide the fact that you prepare your projects with Artisteer. There are people who think that the Artisteer-generated templates are less expensive than the templates made manually or with other tools. Whether they are right or wrong is beyond the scope of this book. If you need, you can change this prefix to anything else.

   ○ You may have an external script operating on specified class names. In such a case, it can be faster to adapt the names in your template code than in the script.

4. The **Additional CSS styles:** field below the **CSS Prefix:** field is a text area, where you can put any additional CSS code you want. This code will be added at the end of the `style.css` file. Unfortunately, there's no support for code writing, like coloring the syntax or at least changing the font, so it's a good idea to prepare your code in an external editor and then paste it here.

5. OK, let's put some code in the **CSS Prefix:** field to realize our task. We want to distinguish images when there is a mouse cursor over them, and controls from the contact from when they are active. Write the following code into this field:

```
/* hover pseudo-class for images
   We use opacity filter */
img:hover
{
  opacity : 0.4;
  filter: alpha(opacity=40);
}

/* and for inputs while they are focused.
   We set their background color as yellow */
input:focus
{
  background-color: yellow;
}
```

6. Click on the **OK** button to close the window and export the template. You will see that our code works successfully as shown in the following screenshot:

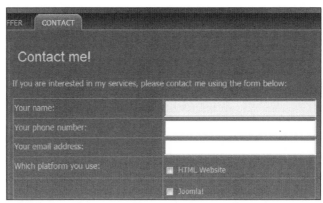

Active input element is distinguished with yellow background

 Actually you don't even have to export the template to observe the changes. Our additional code is interpreted in the Artisteer interface too.

The only problem is that the image effect applies to all the images, not only for those with the Lightbox effect. Well, this is correct, because we defined the hover pseudo class for all the images. To solve this problem, we have to know the class of pictures with the Lightbox effect enabled. Take a look at the source of our home page and you will notice that this class is called img.Lightbox.

7. OK, so let's modify our code:

```
img.art-Lightbox:hover
{
  opacity : 0.4;
  filter: alpha(opacity=40); /* msie */
}

input:focus
{
  background-color: yellow;
}
```

By now our solution works as we planned—we have a roll-over effect for thumbnails of images that have the Lightbox effect active (image gallery), and controls on the contact form are distinguished with a yellow background while they are focused. We have modified the original Artisteer-created `img.art-Lightbox` class and added a pseudo class for active inputs.

8. If you edit the `style.css` file in an exported template, you will see that our code is surrounded with proper comments showing the beginning and end of our modifications.

   While writing code in the **Additional CSS styles:** field is not too comfortable, you may wonder why you should put your code here instead of editing the exported files' code directly, or using your own, additional CSS file. I agree that writing code with any code editor is much more convenient for sure, but you should remember one advantage of using the technique described in this example, and doing it directly in Artisteer also has some advantages. If you put your code directly into Artisteer, your code is stored with the `.artx` project file, which means you don't have to remember about your changes and rewrite them after each export, which is convenient for future changes. That's why I think that if the changes are not too big and you don't have to touch the rest of the exported code, this could be quite a good method.

Another way of modifying CSS files

This tip applies to all kind of templates. An example would be the `OneDayBlue.artx` file.

In the *Styling from scratch* and *Adding additional CSS to the project* tips, we have modified the CSS stylesheets of the relevant project. Each of these examples presents a different approach to the problem:

- We modified an exported CSS template file
- We added some CSS definitions directly in Artisteer

Each of these techniques has its advantages and disadvantages. If you edit the exported CSS file, you can do it with your favorite text editor, which is probably equipped with many tools that make the job more comfortable (like code highlighting). Also, while editing the exported CSS file, you will see all of the content (CSS definitions used in the template) and don't have to write blindfolded. The disadvantage of this approach is that if you modify your project in Artisteer (using GUI) and export the new version once again, your file will be overwritten with the new one, and your modifications will be lost. You will have to rewrite your changes.

If you add CSS directly in Artisteer, your modifications are stored in the .artx project. You can modify the project and export it as many times as you want, and your additional CSS code will be preserved. While this sounds like a better way, the discomfort of writing CSS in Artisteer (with its lack of editorial tools) and the fact that you don't see the rest of the code, makes this really inconvenient.

The third way is to write and save all the modifications in a separate CSS file and then connect it with the rest of the exported files. You can store a copy of your CSS file along with the Artisteer project. If you change something in Artisteer, you can export the project and connect it with your file once again, with minimum effort and time. This way, you can comfortably edit the CSS code with your favorite text editor and you won't lose your work at the next export.

Let's see this technique in practice. Open the example file (OneDayBlue.artx) and take a look at the template. This is just Artisteer's **Blank** template, with only one page and a standard orange title in the header:

Our task is not a surprise. We need to modify the exported CSS files to make this text blue. We do this as follows:

1. Export this template as an HTML template to the OneDayBlue folder and the editstyle.css file. The CSS definition of the site title is:

```
.art-headline,
.art-headline a,
.art-headline a:link,
.art-headline a:visited,
.art-headline a:hover
{
font-size: 36px;
font-family: Arial, 'Arial Unicode MS', Helvetica, Sans-Serif;
font-weight: normal;
font-style: normal;
text-decoration: none;
text-shadow: 0px 2px 3px rgba(0, 0, 0, 0.3);
  padding: 0;
  margin: 0;
  color: #FA6114 !important;
  white-space: nowrap;
}
```

2. To achieve our goal and make the title blue, we need to cover the `color` property. The definition is as follows:

```
.art-headline,
.art-headline a,
.art-headline a:link,
.art-headline a:visited,
.art-headline a:hover
{
  color: blue !important;
}
```

3. We could append the above definition at the end of the `style.css` file. We could type it directly in Artisteer in the **Additional CSS styles:** field by navigating to **Export | Options | CSS Options**. The result is the same and it works (title is blue).

4. Instead of this, let's create a brand new file and call it `myStyles.css`.

5. Write our definition in this file and save it in the exported template folder (`OneDayBlue`). View the site in the browser. Our modification isn't working yet, because we haven't connected our file with the template.

6. To connect our file with the template, edit the `index.html` file. Rather in the beginning of the file, you will find the lines where the CSS files are connected:

```
<!--[if lt IE 9]><script
src="http://html5shiv.googlecode.com/svn/trunk/html5.js"></
script><![endif]-->
<link rel="stylesheet" href="style.css" media="screen">
<!--[if lte IE 7]><link rel="stylesheet" href="style.ie7.css"
media="screen" /><![endif]-->
<link rel="stylesheet" href="style.responsive.css" media="all">
```

7. Under the code given in step 6, add the following line:

```
<link rel="stylesheet" href="myStyles.css" />
```

 The overall pattern when connecting your own CSS file with the web page is `<link rel="stylesheet" href="path-to-your-file" />`

8. Save the file and refresh the site in the browser. Now, when our CSS file is connected to the page, our changes are applied.

If your site contained more than one web page, you would have had to connect your CSS file with every page. Fortunately, in the case of CMS templates, there's usually only one main template file.

9. Using this technique, you should remember several rules, including:

   ○ **Always cover, never remove**: In CSS, every element can be defined many times. Following definitions complement each other. In case of conflict, the last definition has the top priority. Instead of removing a property from the original definition, write this definition once again and cover the particular property with the new value.

   ○ **Connect your CSS file as the last one**: Every page can be connected with many CSS files. In a case where definitions from various files stay in conflict, definitions from the last connected file will have top priority. Connecting your file as the last one gives you confidence that your changes will cover the original definitions generated by Artisteer.

Making a copy of a web page

Sometimes it happens that you need to have an exact copy of an article of a page that you already have in your project. This can be when you want to have several similar pages, differing in some details. Then, instead of manually copying elements one by one, it would be useful to copy the source page, modify the details, and make the next one.

Unfortunately, you can't just select the content of the page with the mouse and then press *Ctrl + C* to copy the content, as that won't work. You can do it within just one cell of content.

The solution is quite simple:

1. Click anywhere within the content area in the page you want to copy from.
2. Click on the **Edit** pane on the ribbon, and then on the **HTML** button in the **Source** group.
3. Check the **Edit whole Article HTML** field.

Check Edit while Article HTML option

4. You will get a warning message that reads **After editing, the content will be combined into one cell**; click on **OK**.

5. Now in the HTML editor you will see all the contents of your page (article). Select the whole text with the mouse (or press *Ctrl + A*), press the right mouse button, and from the content menu choose **Copy** (or just press *Ctrl + C*) to copy the text into the clipboard.

6. Click on the **OK** button to close the HTML editor.

7. Create a new page and click anywhere in the content area.

8. Click on the **HTML** button on the ribbon.

9. Delete everything in the HTML editor and paste the code from the clipboard (press *Ctrl + V*, or press the right mouse button and choose **Paste** from the content menu).

10. Click on the **OK** button to close the HTML editor.

You will notice that the entire content of your source article has been copied.

Adding Lightbox

This tip applies to HTML templates. In case you use a CMS, you should rather use one of the available extensions.

The Lightbox effect is a really cool Artisteer feature that enables you to enrich your projects with image galleries. But Artisteer's Lightbox is not as impressive as the real one. Wouldn't it be nice to have a gallery with the real Lightbox? In this tip, I will show you how to modify the code, to get the gallery with real Lightbox. In this example, we will use the `betterImageGallery.artx` project file.

 Lightbox is the generic name for the group of techniques that display images using modal dialogs. The name comes from original JavaScript plugin, created by *Lokesh Dhakar* (for more information, visit `http://lokeshdhakar.com/projects/lightbox/`). Lightbox-like scripts show images in a nice border, with navigation controls and description text.

We will use the Lightbox2 effect, based on the jQuery library. There are many Lightbox-like effects available, but this one is quite powerful and easy to use. Artisteer uses jQuery for its own Lightbox effect and attaches this library to exported projects by default, so it is a good idea to use an effect based on this library. Here is our procedure:

1. Before we start, we need to prepare some additional files. Artisteer will include the jQuery library, but we need our Lightbox2 effect. You can download it for free from its author website `http://lokeshdhakar.com/projects/lightbox2/`. Go to this page and download the file. This will be a ZIP archive, containing several folders and files. Not all of these files are really needed, but for simplicity just extract the archive. You will get a `Lightbox` folder.

2. The installation package contains not only the necessary files, but also an example page, jQuery library, and some example images. If you want to have only what you really need, you can delete the unnecessary files and keep only the files appearing in the scheme shown in the following screenshot:

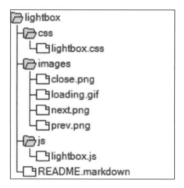

3. The second asset we need are the images we want to show in our gallery. For this example, I have prepared a simple images packet into the ZIP archive. Unzip the `galleryImages.zip` file. You should have the `galleryImages` folder with eight simple images inside.

4. Now, when we have prepared the additional files that we need, start Artisteer and open the `betterImageGallery.artx` project file. You will see that it's just a one-page template, with eight empty cells in the content area. The concept of an image gallery using Lightbox is that the thumbnails of images are displayed on the page. Each thumbnail is a link to the corresponding big image. Without Artisteer, we would need to prepare thumbnails of our images, but we don't have to worry about this, as Artisteer will correctly resize each image while inserting them into cells.

5. Put one image from our collection in each cell. Your project should look similar to the one shown in the following screenshot:

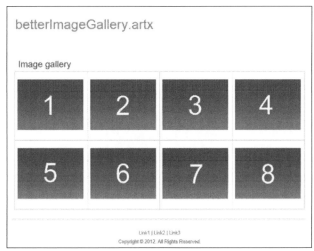

Initial state of our gallery where we have thumbnails in cells in content area

6. Now export the project into a folder, giving it the name `ImageGallery`. Open this folder and double-click on the `index.html` file to view the site in the browser.

7. By default, every picture has the Lightbox effect enabled. Because we are going to replace Artisteer's Lightbox effect with another one, we need to turn it off. Go back to Artisteer, press the right mouse button on every image, choose the **Image Options** option from the content menu, and in the **Image Options** window set the value of the **Preview** field to **No**.

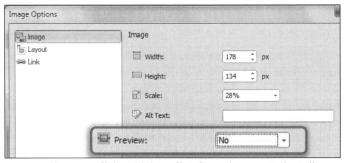

We need to turn off the Lightbox effect for each image in the gallery

8. Export the project once again, under the same name and location, overwriting any previous files.

9. Open this folder and double-click on the `index.html` file to display our site in the browser. Make sure that the Lightbox effect is disabled for any thumbnail in our gallery. If you have missed to disable this effect for any picture, go back to Artisteer, disable it, and export the project one again, overwriting the previously exported files.

10. Open the folder with the exported template and go to the `images` folder. This is the standard Artisteer-generated template folder that contains all the graphic files used in the project. Notice that while inserting the image into our project, Artisteer did not only adopt the size of the original image to the target dimensions (cell), but also made a copy with a thumbnail. We now have two copies of each image of our gallery, that is, a thumbnail (that is actually displayed in cell), and its corresponding image, in the original size. The naming conventions of the generated images are as follows:

Thumbnail	Original image (bigger one)
1.jpg	1-large.jpg
2.jpg	2-large.jpg

   ○ Now it's time for an explanation as to why we had to export the template twice. Any image that we put into the Artisteer project has the **Preview** (the Lightbox effect) property set as **Yes** by default. While we were exporting the project the first time, this option was enabled for all the images. This made Artisteer to create a thumbnail for each image as well as to preserve the original, bigger images (the thumbnail is displayed on the page, and the bigger image is displayed in the Lightbox effect). Then we disabled the Lightbox effect for all the images and exported the project again, overwriting files. If the Lightbox effect is disabled, there is no need to preserve the bigger images, and Artisteer did include them in the exported files. Most of the files were overwritten, but because the location of the exported project didn't change, the old files remained. You may check the date of creation of the files. You will notice that the bigger images are a little older, because they come from our first export, while the smaller ones were overwritten during the second export. With this trick, we have the Lightbox effect disabled, but we still have every image in two versions, as a thumbnail and in its original size.

   ○ Now it's time to transform our thumbnails into links pointing to their corresponding, bigger images.

11. Press the right mouse button on the first image in Artisteer, and from the content menu choose the **Edit Hyperlink...** option. This will open the **Image Options** window with the **Link** tab enabled. In the **Address:** field, we need to type the relative path to the corresponding bigger image of the current thumbnail (take a look at the previous table to check the names of the corresponding images in our gallery).

As all the image are stored in the `images` folder, we need to start the path with the folder name according to the pattern `Folder name/bigger-image-name`.

We are working with the `1.jpg` file (first thumbnail), so in this case, we should type `images/1-large.jpg`.

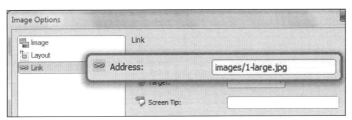

We type the path to the original size image

Repeat this procedure for each image. Export the project again, overwriting the previously exported files.

12. Open our site in the browser. The gallery works, although there's no Lightbox effect yet. When you click on a thumbnail, you are redirected to the page showing the bigger version of image.

If you have problems in this step (after clicking on the thumbnail, there is an error instead of the bigger image being displayed), go back to Artisteer, edit the **Link** properties, and make sure that the value of the **Address:** field doesn't begin with the / character. If so, remove it. For some reason, if the address of a link starts with /, Artisteer adds `.html` to the address. For example:

- right: `images/1-large.jpg`
- wrong: `/images/1-large.jpg`

13. Before we enable the Lightbox2 effect (that will demand us to modify exported code), let's add picture descriptions. Lightbox2 allows you to add a description to the images. Let's assume we want to add the text `This is the first image of our gallery` as the description for the first image.

14. To do that, press the right mouse button on the first thumbnail, and from the content menu select the **Edit Hyperlink…** option again. Then just type your description in the **Screen Tip:** field in the **Image Options** window as shown in the following screenshot:

Adding a description to the image

Repeat the procedure, giving each image an appropriate description.

The last thing we can do in Artisteer is set up a correct `rel` attribute for any link in our gallery. Lightbox2 works only with pictures that have the setting `rel="Lightbox[galleryName]"`.

> This feature makes it possible to have more than one gallery on a page. Each picture is displayed with navigation arrows, allowing the user to switch to the next or previous image. `galleryName` in square brackets identifies the image as belonging to a particular gallery. This name is up to you. If you have more than one gallery on your page, set a proper `galleryName` in `rel` attribute for every image. This will inform Lightbox where a particular gallery ends and where another one starts.

15. To do that, click on any thumbnail and then on the **HTML** button on the ribbon (it's on the **Edit** tab). The HTML editor will appear, presenting the source code of our content area. Look for the link of our first thumbnail (if you're not sure what you are looking for, just look for the thumbnail's filename). Find the fragment of code that looks like the following:

```
<a href="images/1-large.jpg" title="This is the first image of our
gallery">
```

16. Place the cursor to the right of the `title` attribute and add in:

```
rel="Lightbox[myGallery]"
```

17. You should now have the following:

```
<a href="images/1-large.jpg" rel="Lightbox[myGallery]" title="This
is the first image of our gallery">
```

18. Repeat this operation for all the links in our gallery (remember that we have eight images). Click on the **OK** button to close the editor window. Export the project overwriting the previously exported files.

19. The last thing is to modify the exported code and to enrich our site with the real Lightbox effect. Open the folder with the exported project and copy the entire `Lightbox` folder we prepared before to this folder. Then edit the `index.html` file and find the part of the code where jQuery is attached. We are looking for the following line (near the beginning of the file):

```
<script src="jquery.js"></script>
```

20. Just below this line (make some space if needed), put the following code:

```
<!-- we add Lightbox effect -->
<link rel="stylesheet" href="Lightbox/css/Lightbox.css" />
<script src="Lightbox/js/Lightbox.js"/>
<!-- end of our modifications -->
```

21. Save the file and double-click on the `index.html` file. Our gallery should work as expected, but the close and loading images are missing. To fix this, just copy or move the `close.png` and `loading.gif` files from the `Lightbox/images` folder to our `template images` folder (from the `ImageGallery/Lightbox/images` directory to the `ImageGallery/images` directory).

That was the last thing to do. You should now see our project with beautiful, Lightbox2 effect image gallery with smooth display effect, navigation arrows, and image descriptions

Summary

In this chapter, you have learned some tips that allow you to expand the functionality of the generated templates, and to do some things that are not possible from Artisteer directly. While modifying all the exported source code may seem complicated to you, the intention was to show you that automatically generated code can be extended to satisfy custom needs. What's next? Experiment, try to do new things, and don't be afraid. No matter how complicated the task seems to be, all in all it's just HTML. It's also the end of this book. I hope you enjoyed reading it and have found it useful.

Index

Symbols

-blockcontent class 126

A

Academic edition 10
active menu item, horizontal menu 49
Additional CSS styles: field 137
Address: field 145
All Open menu 56
areas 87
art-block Artisteer class 129
articles, content
  writing 62, 63
Artisteer
  about 5
  advanced techniques 90
  CMS system 80-83
  content preparation, advantages 110
  content preparation, disadvantages 110
  customizations 15-17
  footnote, removing 21, 22
  for designer 8
  for hobbyist 8
  for web developer and programmer 9
  for web development company 9
  Home & Academic edition 10
  HTML template 79
  Joomla! templates position, checking 91
  latest version, URL for downloading 10
  new project, creating 11, 12
  program, interface 13
  project, previewing 14
  project, saving 18, 19
  suggestion tool 14

  template 10, 11
  template, exporting 20, 21
  trial version 10
  trial version, to full version 11
  URL 113
  used by 8, 10
  versus other software tools 6, 7
Artisteer-generated classes 133
art-nostyle class 129
artx file 19
attributes, website
  about 24
  colors 27
  layout 27, 28
  one-column layout 28
  page, width 26
  three-column layout 30
  two-column layout 29
  typography 27

B

Background button 32
background, template 38, 39
blank template 31
Block Position 53

C

CMS
  about 79
  content preparation, advantages 110
  content preparation, disadvantages 110
CMS system
  about 80-82
  using 81

Thank you for buying
Creating Templates with Artisteer

About Packt Publishing

Packt, pronounced 'packed', published its first book "*Mastering phpMyAdmin for Effective MySQL Management*" in April 2004 and subsequently continued to specialize in publishing highly focused books on specific technologies and solutions.

Our books and publications share the experiences of your fellow IT professionals in adapting and customizing today's systems, applications, and frameworks. Our solution based books give you the knowledge and power to customize the software and technologies you're using to get the job done. Packt books are more specific and less general than the IT books you have seen in the past. Our unique business model allows us to bring you more focused information, giving you more of what you need to know, and less of what you don't.

Packt is a modern, yet unique publishing company, which focuses on producing quality, cutting-edge books for communities of developers, administrators, and newbies alike. For more information, please visit our website: www.packtpub.com.

Writing for Packt

We welcome all inquiries from people who are interested in authoring. Book proposals should be sent to author@packtpub.com. If your book idea is still at an early stage and you would like to discuss it first before writing a formal book proposal, contact us; one of our commissioning editors will get in touch with you.

We're not just looking for published authors; if you have strong technical skills but no writing experience, our experienced editors can help you develop a writing career, or simply get some additional reward for your expertise.

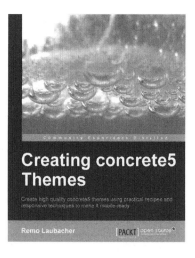

Creating Concrete5 Themes

ISBN: 978-1-78216-164-6   Paperback: 160 pages

Create high quality concrete5 themes using practical recipes and responsive techniques to make it mobile-ready

1. Get to grips with the concrete5 architecture

2. Learn how to create a concrete5 theme

3. Discover how to make a theme responsive to improve it for small devices

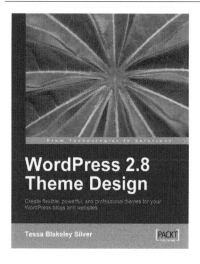

WordPress 2.8 Theme Design

ISBN: 978-1-84951-008-0   Paperback: 292 pages

Create flexible, powerful, and professional themes for your WordPress blogs and websites

1. Take control of the look and feel of your WordPress site by creating fully functional unique themes that cover the latest WordPress features

2. Add interactivity to your themes using Flash and AJAX techniques

3. Expert guidance with practical step-by-step instructions for custom theme design

4. Includes design tips, tricks, and troubleshooting ideas

Please check **www.PacktPub.com** for information on our titles

Made in the USA
San Bernardino, CA
15 July 2013